Talking with Feeling in the Early Years

Early years pedagogy is a deeply human, emotional activity as well as an intellectual and physical one. Drawing on key research, this book explores how 'Work Discussion' can offer a safe space for practitioners to reflect on their daily experience, including the feelings that accompany the work. In facilitating honest and open conversations, it shows how sharing troubling dilemmas and experiences in a supportive environment can improve both the wellbeing of practitioners and the outcomes for children and their families.

This book explains the origins of Work Discussion, the results of a year-long evaluation of its impact in a large early years setting and the accounts of five senior Nursery Leaders who have experienced using Work Discussion. Concluding with practical advice on preparing to go forward for training in facilitating Work Discussion groups in early years settings, chapters cover the following:

- How to set up Work Discussion as a model of professional reflection

- Structuring conversations and responding to difficult incidents and experiences

- The benefits of Work Discussion for practitioners, children, and families

- Detailed case studies of Work Discussion in action

Written by leading experts and including reflective questions throughout, this will be valuable reading for early years practitioners as well as heads, leaders and managers wanting to support their staff's mental health wellbeing.

Peter Elfer is Honorary Research Fellow in the School of Education at the University of Roehampton. He has been Trustee and Chair of Research for the Froebel Trust. His research has been focussed on the experiences of babies, young children, and practitioners in nursery settings.

Talking with Feeling in the Early Years

'Work Discussion' As a Model of Supporting Professional Reflection and Wellbeing

Edited by Peter Elfer

Routledge
Taylor & Francis Group

LONDON AND NEW YORK

Designed cover image: 'Talking and reflecting together in a group' Artwork by
Alice Elfer, photography Sam Elfer

First edition published 2024
by Routledge
4 Park Square, Milton Park, Abingdon, Oxon, OX14 4RN

and by Routledge
605 Third Avenue, New York, NY 10158

Routledge is an imprint of the Taylor & Francis Group, an informa business

British Library Cataloguing-in-Publication Data
A catalogue record for this book is available from the British Library

ISBN: 978-1-032-39338-4 (hbk)
ISBN: 978-1-032-39337-7 (pbk)
ISBN: 978-1-003-34928-0 (ebk)

DOI: 10.4324/b23247

Typeset in Melior
by Apex CoVantage, LLC

Contents

Part three: Nursery Leaders talk about their experience of Work Discussion

Part four: What is involved in leading a Work Discussion group?

Acknowledgements

We would like to acknowledge, with gratitude, a number of organisations and individuals who have been enabling and encouraging of the writing of this book.

First, our thanks goes to Dr. Sacha Powell and the Froebel Trust, who, through encouragement and development and research funding, enabled the year-long research evaluation of Work Discussion. The Trust also funded the establishment of a group for Senior Nursery Leaders to experience Work Discussion and write about their experience in the book. These appear in Part Three of the book.

Next, we would like to thank the early years settings where Heads and leaders supported and made possible the use of Work Discussion. Nursery practitioners from these settings participated with readiness. We recognise how much courage it can take to speak openly about the interactions that a practitioner sometimes found frustrating or confusing in their day-to-day practice. Yet talking about what has been more difficult, as well as what has gone well, is we think a profoundly Froebelian practice and essential to deepening pedagogy.

Lastly, we want to thank the following individuals who, through their particular roles, experiences, and expertise, have made it possible for us to write the book: Michele Barrett, Carole Bromley, Kelly Brooker, Becky Cozens, Katy Dearnley, Julian Grenier, Rachna Joshi, Dawn Rigby, Anita Sawyer, and Sue Smart.

We are deeply appreciative to all those named earlier without whom, of course, the book would not have been possible.

Foreword

Several years ago, in discussion with a close group of early years educators, the question arose of what it means to be 'professional' at work. The most intense part of this conversation revolved around the suggestion from one member of the group that difficult experiences or feelings must be left outside the nursery door. In working with babies or young children, professional identities had emerged through a version of performativity in which kind, caring, thoughtful, sensitive, knowing, thinking – sometimes loving – roles had become normalised and 'positive' expressions of professionalism. In contrast, anxiety, fear, uncertainty, stress, dislike, and disappointment were 'negative' emotions, and there was no room to show or admit to such feelings without risking being judged as 'unprofessional'.

Arguably, all emotions are equally valid – they are different expressions of our human selves as we make the inner outer, to coin a Froebelian expression. How we and others experience different feelings and their effects, and where or how they are permitted to reveal themselves, leads us to qualify some as positive and others as negative. In families, communities, and societies, the whole gamut of emotions is universal; but their acceptability (or not) is socially constructed. The whole point of a horror movie is to make us feel fear or revulsion, and we are expected to scream in terror. The expression of these feelings is acceptable in context. Throughout life, we learn what is socially and contextually acceptable to reveal of our emotional selves. And so we often decide – or are made to feel – that certain feelings must remain hidden from children and from the adults we work with. It is as though one half of our emotional human selves has been erased. We are shiny, happy people.

I am not advocating a lack of self-regulation and outpourings of emotions to children or adults at any time at work. Nor am I trying to downplay the importance of naming negative feelings and their consequences, especially when support is needed. But I am suggesting the value in recognising that feelings like distress or loathing are an everyday part of human life and that automatically referring to them as negative diminishes their situatedness. They are biological responses to how we perceive or imagine something that is happening to us or around us.

This book is an exploration of this *situatedness of feelings* and particularly those that are so often seen as negative in the professional context of early childhood education.

Where it is unusual, taboo, or 'unprofessional' to express particular emotions, this book tells courageous stories from the heart and soul of early years experience where educators have engaged in a process of Work Discussion. The contributors demonstrate how honesty about feelings is hard. But when these truths are nurtured in an atmosphere that welcomes and works with openness as part of transformative professional reflection, it can strengthen the whole team.

> Whenever our emotional responses erupt, many of us believe our academic purpose has been diminished. To me this is really a distorted notion of . . . practice, since the underlying assumption is that to be truly intellectual we must be cut off from our emotions.

(Hooks, 1994, p. 155)
Sacha Powell, 29 June 2023

Reference

Hooks, b. (1994) *Teaching to transgress. Education as the practice of freedom.* London: Routledge.

General introduction

What this book is about

This book is about a safe space in which nursery staff can think through the ups and downs of daily nursery relationships. It is a place in which staff can 'say it like it is'.

The safe space described in the book is called 'Work Discussion'. Work Discussion is a carefully organised time in which professionals, using relationships as part of their work, can talk about and try to untangle the knots that always occur in work relationships.

Work Discussion has a long history. It has been used by many different professional groups, including doctors and psychologists, teachers and social workers, nurses, and probation officers. This book is about Work Discussion for nursery professionals – early years pedagogues.

'Work Discussion' is not a very exciting name, but the way it works, the kind of talking and thinking it encourages, and the help it provides is exciting.

Why this book matters

Nursery work must be one of the most misunderstood and undervalued professional roles. How many nursery professionals have been told what a cushy job they have 'just playing with children all day'. Throughout the education system, the rule of thumb appears to be that the younger the child, the easier and more basic is the work. Working with babies is the easiest of all – little more than feeding and cleaning. We know the science tells a completely different story, a story of how much the earliest months and years matter. Our own human experience also tells a completely different story.

Working with the babies and young children of others needs professional preparation. Practitioners are asked to manage complicated challenges, for example, helping each child feel loved and thought about whilst treating all children equally and keeping to professional boundaries. We say more about these challenges in the

Introduction on page xx. Practitioners are making judgements about this, and other challenges, all the time, often on their own and as they work. It is important though to have the opportunity to explore your judgements and thinking about your work relationships with other nursery practitioners and be able to hear how they see things. The book matters because managing these professional relationships well is vital for babies and young children, and Work Discussion is a way of helping each practitioner to do that.

Who the book is for

This is NOT a book only for new or inexperienced nursery practitioners. It is for ALL nursery practitioners, however high their qualifications, however long their experience. If a practitioner says they do not need any time for professional reflection or that they do it on their own, we think they are at risk of not being as helpful to children as they could be. We also think they are not being fair to themselves. They are as entitled to the support and feedback of others working with young children as much as anyone else.

What the book covers

The book first explains what Work Discussion is. It is a safe space to talk, think about, and strengthen professional relationships at work. As importantly, the book explains what Work Discussion is not. For example, it is not therapy! It is not a space to off-load personal worries, and it is not a space to have a competition with others in the group about who copes best with the work.

The book then describes a research evaluation of Work Discussion in nurseries, what the practitioners participating thought about it, and how it supported children's progression.

The third section is made up of five 'stories', written by five Senior Nursery Leaders of their experience of being in a Work Discussion group.

The final section is about how you might begin to think about leading a Work Discussion group.

What will you gain from reading the book?

Like the old joke, if you want to get fit, you need to do more than join a gym. You have to go to the gym and work out too! Learning about Work Discussion is important, and this book will help you do that. But it will not do much to deepen your practice or help you manage your work better, unless you use the book as a springboard to participate in a Work Discussion group! That is the hard part. But we think it is the part that will help you manage the work better, offer a deeper pedagogy to the children and families with whom you work, and will make your experience of the work more satisfying.

PART ONE
Relationships matter

Feelings and emotions in nursery relationships

Introduction to part one

The feelings and emotions we are talking about in this book are the feelings that are part and parcel of the ordinary daily interactions that nursery practitioners have with colleagues, children, and families.

These feelings include ordinary positive human feelings, for example, love, joy, satisfaction. They also include ordinary negative human feelings, for example, hurt, sadness, worry, frustration, and sometimes anger.

In our experience, nursery practitioners talk easily about the positive feelings they experience in their daily work. However, practitioners seem much less ready to talk about the negative feelings they have. This is understandable! It is much easier to talk about what is going well rather than what has been difficult. We think, too, that many practitioners are worried, perhaps from experience, that others will criticise them if they admit to struggling with their work in some way, for example, finding it difficult to work with an individual child or adult. Maybe they have been told that it is unprofessional to feel like that or that they will be seen as not coping with the work as everyone else 'seems' to be (although many others may be covering up their own difficult feelings with the work). However, we have never come across a nursery practitioner, whether senior or junior, highly qualified or completely unqualified, who has not felt some negative emotions during their nursery day. When a team can share the common or different difficulties each member experiences, alongside the joys and satisfactions of the work, the team will be much stronger.

Struggles in the work may arise from a baby, child, or adult who somehow gets under a practitioner's skin, although the practitioner is not sure why. It may be something that has upset them during the day, for example, an interaction that seems to follow a familiar pattern of interactions that is upsetting or frustrating.

Human beings are unique communicators. We listen and try and understand what others are telling us with words and body language. We are also able to evoke feelings in others, in the ways in which we communicate with them. We know that babies and young children learn to do this from very early on, as a result of their interactions with others. It is part of the way they can communicate to us, without

DOI: 10.4324/b23247-1

words, what they are feeling. For babies who have no words yet, it is especially important that practitioners try and read their behaviour and understand it.

The nursery practitioner can then model a conversation in which they ask the baby or child to 'tell me what you are so cross and upset about'. Then offering possible reasons, the practitioner helps young children to express and communicate their feelings rather than only being able to do this by actions or by yelling.

All these feelings, both positive and negative, are at the heart of pedagogic interactions and relationships. However, sometimes understanding meanings and managing interactions, especially when you are immersed in them, is not easy. We think practitioners need a place in which they can talk and think about their interactions, together with the positive and negative feelings that accompany them, with other nursery practitioners. We think that if all these different feelings can be expressed, without fear of criticism, and be understood, then two key benefits will come from the time invested. The first is a deeper pedagogy in which children's feelings are better understood and responded to. The second is a more satisfying and less stressful experience for the practitioners themselves. This book is about Work Discussion as one model of professional reflection in which these two benefits can potentially be achieved.

The 2022 Froebel Trust Annual Lecture was called 'Telling Stories about Radical Change and Belonging'. It was given by the acclaimed choreographers and performers Anthony and Kel Matsena. The lecture is on the Trust website, which describes the brothers:

> talk about their childhood, their family life and their experience of moving to Wales as children. They speak about how dance, music and creativity were an integral part of their family life from a very young age – 'Dance was a way we could untangle the things we were experiencing when we didn't have the language to express what we were feeling'.

Following their lecture, Professor Tina Bruce, Honorary Professor of Early Education at the University of Roehampton, was the first respondent. She said:

> you are making safe nurturing spaces for the people who work with you. . . . it leads to facing, rather than avoiding, the painful . . . the things that cannot be easily spoken about . . . it's VERY Froebelian.

Work Discussion is a safe, nurturing space for nursery practitioners to talk about the painful and difficult aspects of pedagogic interactions as well as the joyful and rewarding aspects. This is the essence of Work Discussion. Thus, in the way that Tina Bruce has stated, we can think of Work Discussion as an essential Froebelian practice

In Chapter 1, Peter Elfer talks about the importance of feelings in early years practice and how we think they have been taken rather for granted.

In Chapter 2, Dilys Wilson talks about the development of Work Discussion as a model of professional reflection in the early years.

Let's get serious about feelings in early years practice

Peter Elfer

In this chapter, we look at the following:

- Relationships matter in nursery practice, and feelings are part of all pedagogic relationships.
- Nursery practitioners' feelings are often taken for granted. This puts at risk effective pedagogy and practitioner wellbeing.
- When feelings can be talked about and thought about, deeper pedagogy for children and families takes place and practitioner satisfaction and wellbeing is nurtured.

Relationships matter in nursery practice, and feelings are part of all pedagogic relationships

Relationships, and the feelings that make relationships alive, are of the utmost importance for all of us but for children especially. Feelings are at the heart of nursery practice; we could say they ARE the heart of nursery practice. Robots may be able to take over many jobs. They could never take over as nursery practitioners.

Friedrich Froebel knew about relationships and feelings in one of the best ways to 'know' about anything. He had experienced for himself, as a young child, how much relationships matter. In the following quotation, he describes the deep feelings of losing his mother and gaining a stepmother:

> I reached my fourth year. My father then married again and gave me a second mother. My soul must have felt deeply at this time the want of a mother's love – parental love -for in this year occurs my first consciousness of self. I remember that I received my new mother overflowing with feelings of simple and faithful child-love towards her. These sentiments made me happy,

DOI: 10.4324/b23247-2

developed my nature and strengthened me because they were kindly received and reciprocated by her.[1]

Froebel then describes in his autobiography how his stepmother had her own baby and became very cold to him. He speaks of his loneliness and grief. It is heartrending to read. However, Froebel shows us, like much else in his writing and teaching learned from first-hand experience, the deep importance of relationships and feelings in relationships:

> To the child the sight of the grown-ups around him – and this is very true of his parents who at first command his whole field of vision – is the sun which draws him out; and when he establishes other relationships within and beyond himself, these are the climatic conditions, the broad sky, under which he grows up.
>
> (Lilley, 1967, p. 78)

Adults at home and at nursery, in the relationships they form with children, are the 'sun' that draws them out! 'Relationships matter' has now become one of the Froebel Trust's eight 'Froebelian principles'.

200 years later, Froebel's deep understanding of these connections has been shown in modern research:

> Why do infants, indeed all people, so strongly seek states of interpersonal connectedness and why does the failure to achieve connectedness wreak such damage on their emotional, mental, and physical health?
>
> (Tronick, 2005, p. 293)

Jools Page, in her ground-breaking work on 'Professional Love' (Page, Clare and Nutbrown, 2013), has shown how much mothers expect and want nursery practitioners to 'love' their babies and young children, a very special and close form of 'interpersonal connectedness'.

From the practitioners' point of view, enabling all children to feel this interconnectedness is very demanding work. Feeling so closely emotionally involved, within clear professional boundaries, in the lives of babies and young children can be immensely rewarding and satisfying. However, as well as being so satisfying, it can *also* be stressful and demanding. Practitioners have to work hard to manage all the feelings the work involves. It is about helping all the children feel loved and responded to, although the practitioner may not always feel this to all the children! It is also, and at the same time, about being professional and not getting too involved or too distant. It is about sensitivity to parents' feelings. And it is about practitioners managing their own ordinary human feelings of sadness and loss as children move on from one room to an older age group room in nursery or from nursery to school.

I have spent nearly all my career, from starting out to retirement, as a researcher in nurseries, watching how nursery practitioners work with babies and young children. It would be impossible not to see and feel the joy that is part of these interactions and how much the children gain. This is not the whole story, though. The work is also intensely demanding. It can feel overwhelming just to listen and observe as a researcher, never mind actually doing the work as a practitioner. The work takes energy, and it takes cleverness and an ability to think through and make judgements. Nursery work is hard work, physically and intellectually. The foundation of this book, though, is that nursery work is hard work emotionally too. I think that emotional work needs recognising and supporting.

Nursery practitioners' feelings are often taken for granted. This puts effective pedagogy and practitioner wellbeing at risk

Nursery practitioners are using their feelings all the time in their work. They use them in welcoming children, in helping children with their own feelings during the day, and in sensing how children are experiencing their day in nursery.

We see this use of feelings, even when it may seem to the individual practitioner as natural and spontaneous, as a vital part of their pedagogic work. It may seem strange to talk about feelings that nursery practitioners show, and sometimes hold back, as 'work'. Many nursery practitioners have told us that they think of their warmth and care towards the children as 'just part of the job'. They may say, 'Oh, it just comes naturally', or 'I don't think of it as work'. In many ways, this is perhaps how it should be. We might think a practitioner who says s/he is working hard all the time to show s/he cares is perhaps in the wrong job! Yet many practitioners have told us how emotionally exhausted they can feel at the end of the week or even at the end of the day. The American sociologist Arlie Hochschild has described this work with feelings as emotional labour. She refers to it as a 'third' form of labour at work, alongside physical labour and intellectual labour.

I have always felt impressed and moved by the huge reservoirs of affection, empathy, joy, patience, care, and love that nursery practitioners demonstrate. Yet I also know from practitioners that unwinding at home, after a demanding day, can be difficult. I think their work with feelings is justifiably described as 'emotional labour'.

How do practitioners manage this emotional labour, the work they do with children's emotions and their own emotions, perhaps almost without thinking? It seems to me very unhelpful, as I have sometimes heard, to describe nursery practitioners as 'angels' or 'born to the work' as if, however enjoyable and satisfying it is at times, their work comes without effort and without costs. By 'costs', I mean tiredness, exhaustion, and stress. Some practitioners describe how they deal with these costs by off-loading to partners, family, or friends. Most people spend some time doing that at the end of some days.

Nevertheless, early years work involves serious *emotional* work and letting go of all the feelings that have built up on certain days may take time and a lot of talking through. If you are reading this as a nursery practitioner, you may feel you do not need any reminding of the emotional demands of the job. However, if you are not a nursery practitioner, just look again at what is expected, just in the first part of the day. That is when babies, children, and families are arriving. Some will be over-joyed to be arriving at nursery, but for others, the separation may be painful and the role of the nursery practitioner in helping them, and their caregivers, manage this transition is vital work.

Settling in a new baby or child, new to nursery and distressed at having to part from the person who has brought them, is hard work. It requires the practitioner to be able to find some space in their minds, even if they cannot do this for long, to be available to that child. Robyn Dolby, working with nursery practitioners in Australia, has developed the idea of *Playspaces* (Dolby, Hughes and Friezer, 2013). *Playspaces* is rooted in the minutiae of how educators greet children and receive their feelings.

Robyn's aim is to create room for the practitioners to think about the children and what they may be communicating and feeling and to think about their own feelings in response to the children. The way practitioners attend to children's feelings contributes in large part to how children and families feel welcomed and included (accepting all the feelings of each child), how children feel known (knowing each child's individual ways of expressing feelings), and responding to children's sense of equity (their experience that everyone is seen and appreciated, each person's feelings seen and understood with receptive rather than critical eyes).

Some babies and children manage to settle easily, forming a good relationship with a practitioner, and soon being able to enjoy being at nursery with all that it offers. It is not like this, though, for every baby and child. Their distress is painful to witness, which perhaps explains why some parents want to leave quietly without saying goodbye or why some practitioners resort so quickly to distraction before a child is ready to be part of the nursery community. It is enormously complex and demanding work for practitioners, especially when they have many other children arriving.

I have focussed on feelings at the beginning of the nursery day when babies and children are arriving and are separating from their loved family adults. This is only the beginning, even if it may set the tone for the rest of the day. There are feelings to be considered throughout the day. And at the other end of the nursery day, when everyone – children, parents, and practitioners – are tired and perhaps rushed, there is the process of saying goodbye and, this time, the separation from the loved nursery adults and the task of settling back into home routines. Finally, when children are moving onto an older age group room or onto another setting, practitioners must manage their sadness at saying goodbye to children of whom they have become fond and to whom they are now attached. We have heard some more senior practitioners say that managing these emotions becomes easier with experience. Yet in Part Three of the book, five Senior Nursery Leaders, with decades of experience between them, all refer in their 'stories' to the feelings of attachment and loss they still must carefully manage, rather than deny or avoid thinking about them and trying to understand them.

Is it enough to 'off-load' to family and friends at the end of difficult days? Perhaps this is just an ordinary part of anyone's working life, to share enjoyable as well as more difficult interactions that have been part of their working day. Yet for nursery practitioners, where interactions ARE the working day, I think it is not enough to rely on family and friends who probably do not have experience of nursery work themselves and may not be able to understand the complexities and intensity of it (and family and friends will perhaps end up feeling a bit fed up themselves). I do not think nursery practitioners can work sensitively with feelings if their 'feelings work', (emotional labour), is simply taken for granted. I think if practitioners' feelings are taken for granted, as if needing no special thought and understanding, how can we expect practitioners to endlessly attend to children's feelings, thinking about them and understanding them, as part of their pedagogic work?

When feelings can be talked about and thought about, deeper pedagogy for children and families happens and practitioner satisfaction and wellbeing is nurtured

You may have come across a saying 'least said, soonest mended'. When I have asked nursery practitioners about how they manage the emotional demands of their work, especially when it has been a tough day, they often play down how tough it has been. They may say something like 'Oh you just have to laugh it off and move on!'

When something has gone wrong at work, it may indeed feel best to shrug it off, hoping that no one, other than you, has noticed too much and that everyone will soon forget it. When practitioners are in the middle of a working day, they have no choice but to put difficult feelings to one side. Our argument in this book is that, as tempting as this may be, it is not the best way forward. An incident with a child, parent, or colleague may happen more than once. There may be a feeling that things always get awkward or tense with a particular person. You may feel that when in that situation, someone does something that leaves you feeling the same negative feelings inside. It can be very wearing and annoying.

Shrugging it off can seem an attractive option. The danger of shrugging something off is there is likely to be meaning behind the interaction that is never looked at or thought about. A nursery Key Person told us about the close attachment she had formed with a 2-year-old girl, Alison, and how excited Alison was to see her in the mornings. When Alison's mother was expecting a new baby, the Key Person had worked especially hard with the mother to help prepare Alison. However, when the baby arrived, Alison arrived in nursery refusing to have anything to do with the Key Person. The Key Person felt mystified that she should be rejected at a time when she thought she would be needed most. She also felt a little hurt but understood, too, that for a young child, the arrival of a baby sister or brother is unsettling.

However, when the Key Person talked with her manager about Alison's behaviour, they wondered together if Alison was making the Key Person feel what she was feeling at that time – a sense of rejection and being unwanted. In other words, Alison was 'acting out' the feelings she felt but was not able to put into words. When the Key Person understood this and could talk with Alison about it, Alison's behaviour gradually changed, and she returned to being the loving, playful child who, of course, still needed the Key Person's careful attention.

In general, feelings are part of all interactions and relationships, and this is so important for nursery practitioners to seek to understand because this understanding contains the child's more difficult feelings that lie beneath the surface and are, therefore, not accessible to the child. This 'understanding what is being communicated by feelings' is the role of Work Discussion. It is about not only looking at what's on the surface but also at how and why the child's feelings are being expressed in this way. A practitioner who feels a child's behaviour has changed or is disturbed by the child's behaviour but does not understand why or how to address it might bring it to a Work Discussion group to be thought about.

As you think about the impact of feelings in your work, let me ask you, the reader, if you have been surprised by how deeply you have been affected by an interaction at work which you feel should not have affected you as much as it did. Sometimes when someone cannot bear the feelings they are having, they push them away into us. We may in ordinary terms feel 'dumped on'. For babies and young children, this process of communicating the feelings they cannot manage themselves is very important. It is a way for them to alert others, perhaps alongside crying, that they are struggling. They make adults, for example, their parents, other family adults, and nursery practitioners, feel stirred up and concerned. Parents and family members, hopefully, are able to use these feelings and think about their meaning – what is wrong with my baby or child and how can I address what has happened (for example, tiredness, crossness, hunger, physical pain, sadness) – and help them sort it out if it can be sorted out, or at least that their feelings are understood if it cannot be sorted out.

For nursery practitioners doing this with many different children from different backgrounds, thinking about the meaning of what is stirred up inside themselves is much more challenging. It is not necessarily easy to manage alone. The message of this book, and the role of Work Discussion, is that nursery practitioners need, and should be entitled to, a space away from their children, where they can give one another the support to do that talking and understanding together. We think this is important for effective pedagogy and important for practitioner wellbeing and job satisfaction.

International frameworks (Urban *et al.*, 2012) and the national policies of many countries and individual organisations (OECD, 2017) include the requirement that early years systems of organisation and practice must do more to support the early years workforce if nursery practitioners are to be fully responsive to the emotional needs of the children.

Nurseries today are generally well organised, and safety standards are high. Nevertheless, the emotional demands of working closely with young children can still be intense. If we can recognise and support this emotional labour as a vital part of the complex work that nursery practitioners undertake, then pedagogy might be more rewarding, and the loss of skilled practitioners to the profession through exhaustion and burnout be reduced.

My experience has been that most nursery practitioners are nothing other than committed and deeply caring towards the wellbeing and development of young children in their care. But no one can do this work endlessly, with sensitivity and emotional engagement, if there are not the 'permitting circumstances' of doing it well (enough staff, decent pay and conditions, ongoing training), and regular and frequent opportunities to think about and understand the complex interactions that are the heart of the work.

Note

1 Friedrich Fröbel Emilie Michaelis Mme. *Autobiography of Friedrich Froebel* (Translated and annotated by E. Michaelis & Moore, H.K.). 1886 (Joint tr.). Print Book 1915 [12th ed.]. London, Allen & Unwin, 1915. Page 4.

2 Introducing Work Discussion as an holistic model of professional reflection

Dilys Wilson

In this chapter, we look at the following:

- Why professional reflection is important and the value of reflecting with others.

- What is Work Discussion? A forum for nursery practitioners to think with colleagues about the children and families they work with in which particular attention is given to both the positive and negative feelings that may be stirred up through their work.

- The development of Work Discussion as a model of professional reflection and its first applications in nurseries.

- The dilemmas, uncertainties, and unexpected feelings arising from day-to-day practice.

Why professional reflection is important and the value of reflecting with others

The importance of professional reflection for nursery practitioners is widely agreed across research, curriculum, and policy literature. In England, for example, the Early Years Foundation Stage (EYFS) requires practitioners to 'reflect on the different rates at which children are developing and adjust their practice appropriately' (DfES, 2021, p. 16) so that they can be responsive to each child's learning and developmental journey. Inspection frameworks expect nurseries to use evaluation to illustrate the effectiveness of their practice and for practitioners to talk knowledgably about their pedagogical approach. But to create the conditions for this to happen, opportunities to reflect with others on observations of children can help us to question our assumptions and gain new insights. This resonates with a Froebelian approach where the holistic needs and play interests of the children are kept firmly at the centre of nursery practice, and reflection is recognised as a

DOI: 10.4324/b23247-3

key to understanding each unique child. Tovey (2020) argues that using Froebel's principles in practice today:

> requires critical reflection, discussion, and a willingness to question taken for granted ideas. In challenging times, we need strong advocates for young children, their families, and communities so that together we can work towards shaping a better future.
>
> (Tovey, 2020)

It falls on leaders and managers to create the conditions for reflective practice to flourish. Building a culture of reflection and discussion that will motivate and enrich everyone involved in each unique nursery environment is an important pedagogical aspiration.

Practitioners working in nursery settings will be familiar with balancing the 'in-the-moment' needs and demands of different children, families, and colleagues. In these busy environments, making quick decisions on the best course of action to take to navigate an unfolding sequence of events is a common experience. Babies and young children thrive in close relationships with practitioners who know them well and in environments where there are opportunities to play and enjoy interactions with others. The backdrop to their involvement in play and their relationships with others is the practitioners' capacity to be curious about each child's learning interests and development and to help children to recognise and express their feelings, which in turn helps them to regulate their behaviour.

Schön (1983) wrote that professionals manage these experiences at work through their 'knowledge-in-action' arising from the professional knowledge they have gained through training and on-the-job experience. Schön also used the term 'reflection-in-action' to describe the on-the-spot decisions that are made and acted upon in practice as they happen. This concept is often used to help nursery practitioners to be aware, as they interact with children and notice what they are communicating verbally or through their play, of how they behave and what that suggests about what they want to do and how they are feeling. This 'in-action' reflection is an important part of a wider reflective process that also involves 'reflection-on-action' – that is, when away from the immediate demands of the children, to actively think with colleagues about the experience of a particular interaction. Most practitioners in their work seem to have had the experience of an interaction where they feel they have not understood something in a child's response, or of feeling puzzled or unsettled or upset by something that has happened in their work. Work Discussion is a model of reflection is one of many that tries to unpick how professionals use knowledge in practice and how reflection plays a part in enhancing on-the-job learning and expertise. Referring to Schön's model, 'Work Discussion' offers an opportunity to 'reflect-on-action' in the company of others, but it also draws on a wider theoretical approach to learning from experience that considers the way *we feel* as well as what *we know*.

What is 'Work Discussion'?

The ordinary work dilemmas that arise for professionals whose roles involve close caring and nurturing, teaching, or supporting relationships with others can generate emotions that linger or are difficult to think through and understand alone. 'Work Discussion' is a model of group reflection that takes note of the descriptive detail of work interactions and relationships, but it also focuses on a practitioner's subjective experience, including their emotional responses. Nursery practice routinely involves noticing and actively responding to the different ways that babies and young children express their emotions. Helping a child to manage their feelings by providing positive support and encouragement can be enjoyable and satisfying, but more difficult feelings get stirred up, too, and can be hard to think about. Thinking about our own feelings as we work with children may not be a familiar strategy to use, but doing so can offer additional ways of understanding why we find some situations harder to manage than others. Deepening pedagogical practice involves being able to be more open about the presence of personal feelings and how they are an integral part of professional work with young children.

The ethos of a Work Discussion group is to provide a reflective space for the group members to share an observation or speak about a work situation that they would like to explore further. This could be a dilemma or an interesting, surprising, or confusing scenario that would benefit from further attention and reflection:

> we all notice so much more than we realise – not only about what is going on in the external world, but what is going on inside our minds – thoughts and feelings – and our bodies.
>
> (Jackson and Klauber, 2018, p. 245)

A small group of around six members is an ideal number for a Work Discussion group, but depending on the context, for example, with larger staff teams in nurseries or as part of a training programme, group numbers may be higher. The agreed schedule of meetings, either weekly, fortnightly, or monthly, with a clear time limit of around 60–90 minutes, helps to establish a reflective space for one or more presenters to talk about the often knotty problems and complicated feelings that arise from work situations. The purpose of Work Discussion is not to provide therapy for the group but to acknowledge that strong personal feelings and authentic compassion are an integral and holistic part of professional relationships with children and families. Facilitators who understand the professional context of the group and have experience of supporting Work Discussion groups pay close attention to the content of the presenter's observation or summary of their scenario. By prompting the presenter and the wider group to explore their thoughts and associations and by responding in ways that avoid any false reassurance or platitudes, facilitators are able to model ways of reflecting together in a professional context that encourages greater empathy. The organisation and facilitation of Work Discussion groups provide the conditions for reflective discussions to emerge without fear of judgement or criticism.

Work Discussion groups were developed by the Tavistock Centre[1] for training purposes, drawing on an understanding of the impact of the thoughts and feelings that exist beneath the surface for us all. The Tavistock Centre has a long tradition of exploring the impact of the hidden emotional factors that influence the way we learn and relate to each other. As individuals, and collectively when working in groups or within organisations, there are occasions when situations or relationships become difficult for us to manage and cause additional stress and anxiety. When these feelings surface at work, in order to cope in a professional way and avoid feeling overwhelmed, we all have our own ways, even if we are not conscious of them, of trying to avoid these feelings to protect ourselves. As Elfer (2012, p. 133) points out, these 'ordinary human defences may lead professionals to avoid aspects of their work that they experience as upsetting or anxiety provoking'.

Grappling with uncertainty and not knowing is an integral part of the process of thinking. Unsurprisingly, there are a number of pitfalls in trying to think about and put into words the emotional impact of uncomfortable situations and the feelings that get stirred up. This challenge also manifests itself in a Work Discussion group experience, as the content of the discussion often draws attention to the 'elephant in the room', or the parts of a story that have not been explicitly included. Many people will have experienced how deeply one can be affected, perhaps almost overwhelmed, by the strong feelings of someone else, even when nothing may have been said openly. Feelings can be 'put into us' by another. This can be understood as a means of communicating through feeling states. It is helpful to know that this can happen when trying to make sense of our own emotional responses, especially when we are surprised by a strong reaction that may be out of keeping with our usual character.

In early years practice, practitioners routinely respond to children to help them to manage the strong feelings that they are struggling with and expressing through their behaviour. Thoughtful responses and carefully timed interactions provide the children with an emotionally holding experience that helps to reassure them, but the relentless nature for practitioners of providing this emotional support is often draining. Children need these reassuring relationships to thrive in a nursery environment, but practitioners also need opportunities to express their own feelings and reflect on what they notice about children's distress. If these first thoughts and feelings have no space to be considered, they can get in the way of an attuned response to challenging behaviour. The process of having the support of other people to think clearly about what might have been a confusing or even an overwhelming experience is helpful, and this experience is something that we can all benefit from regardless of age or stage of development.

Work Discussion offers this opportunity to attend to the emotions that are evoked from work with children in nurseries. The group itself, with the support of the facilitators, offers a place to think together and feel more 'contained'.

The development of Work Discussion as a model of professional reflection and its first applications in nurseries

The Work Discussion model described previously has been applied to meet the needs of different groups of professionals, including nursery practitioners, through Continuing Professional Development (CPD) opportunities or as work supervision. Juliet Hopkins, a senior Child Psychotherapist, using her training, was one of the first to offer support to nursery practitioners, helping them to think about relationships with children and families. She helped them draw out some of their feelings about the work and, in particular, what upset and worried them as well as what they enjoyed.

She did this work in the early 1980s (Hopkins, 1988), when many nurseries fell under the umbrella of Social Services, providing support for families from disadvantaged backgrounds. Places in these nurseries were allocated to babies and young children from families facing particular difficulties or if there were concerns about their development or behaviour. But there was a growing awareness of the challenges involved in meeting the emotional needs of children within this system of provision. Research at the time had found that practitioners often focussed on the physical health and development of the babies and young children, but they tended to avoid establishing the close relationships and consistent attention that would support the children's emotional development and wellbeing. Hopkins recognised the urgency of finding a way to help practitioners to understand and connect with the emotional needs of the children in their care, but she also wanted to find out more about what interfered with their capacity to do this in practice. She was surprised that practitioners who had chosen to work with babies and young children and had received training to do so found it so difficult to keep the children's emotional needs in mind.

Hopkins's intention for the group of practitioners she worked with was to achieve a shift in perception about their relationships and interactions with the children. She did this by discussing with them themes on attuned care, emotional development, and attachment relationships, alongside the practitioners' own choice of discussion topics. This approach enabled her to use the group discussions to help the practitioners reflect on their practice so that they could begin to notice and talk about the emotional challenges that they faced in their daily work with the babies, children, and their families.

Hopkins's findings showed that creating a non-judgemental space was helpful for the practitioners to communicate their thoughts and feelings. This approach was very different from their previous experience of any kind of professional training, and they were relieved that Hopkins respected their professionalism and wanted to listen carefully to what they said and what was worrying them in their day to day work.

The group leaders made it clear that they were there to help the group to learn from each other and to find their own solutions to problems, rather than to tell them what to do.

(Hopkins, 1988, p. 108)

Although the practitioners understood why attachment relationships were important, during the discussions, they were able to explore the conflict between this ideal of enabling emotional attachments between nursery staff and the children (what we would call the Key Person relationship today), and the messier reality of managing close relationships and emotional ties with children in practice. Talking about these experiences and sharing how they felt helped them to connect more with their own emotional experience which in turn made it easier for them to understand the children's emotional needs. As the discussions progressed, Hopkins noticed that most practitioners who participated became more able to share thoughtful observations of the children's emotional needs and to discuss ways of supporting them. The more challenging aspect of this new awareness for them was that they also began to appreciate the impossible task of being able to fully meet the needs of those children who had experienced trauma or other early adverse circumstances. This paradox illustrates the complex range of feelings that exist together for those working professionally with babies and young children and the importance of having systems of support to be able to make sense of unsettling feelings.

At the time of Hopkins's Work Discussions with her group of practitioners, the importance of attachment relationships for children's emotional development had been recognised and a new system of allocating children to a named practitioner was in the process of being introduced in the nurseries where the practitioners were working. This shift in policy illustrates the timeliness of Hopkins's input and the importance for the practitioners of having had the support they received from being able to talk openly: dilemmas, uncertainties, and unexpected feelings were experienced and could be explored, as they found ways of adapting to a very different way of working.

The dilemmas, uncertainties, and unexpected feelings arising from day-to-day practice

In Chapter 1, Peter Elfer talked about how readily nursery practitioners talk about the positive and pleasurable aspects of their work – the joy and satisfaction, for example, but how much harder it seemed for them to talk about what was more difficult about the work. Nursery practitioners have often said family and friends think that their work is easy, 'just playing with children all day'. What is it about the work that makes this image so wrong and demeaning?

Table 2.1 Dilemmas raised by the practitioners in the discussions with Juliet Hopkins

- The loss they experienced when a child they were close to left the nursery.
- How to respond to what they thought were excessive demands for attention from children who were attached to them since they were worried about 'spoiling' them by giving them the attention they wanted.
- Concerns about making a child's mother jealous of the affectionate relationship that they, the practitioner, had developed with the child.
- Feeling that they ought to treat all children equally but feeling guilty when they realised that they were drawn to some children more than others.
- Fears about the impact on the child and family for a child experiencing a closer relationship with them at nursery than they had at home.

Source: Hopkins, 1988

With this in mind, it is interesting to look back at the issues that the practitioners talked to Juliet Hopkins about. Through the group discussions, they had been able to connect with their feelings about working in a more intimate way with the children, and Table 2.1 illustrates the more difficult dilemmas that they chose to talk about.

It is very noticeable that all these dilemmas are about the impact of professional relationships with children and families that involve difficult and conflicting personal feelings. It is unsurprising that without sufficient support, each of these dilemmas could become overwhelming and cause upset and confusion. Intimacy involves our most basic feelings, and our own past experiences will surface in one way or another to influence our responses. Knowing about this and accepting it as part of professional practice in our relationships with babies and young children does not reduce the intensity of these feelings. However, being able to talk about them and appreciate that we all have different ways of coping with the feelings we have, although difficult, is because it enables us to gain insight into these feelings and where they come from.

When Juliet Hopkins talked to nursery practitioners about their work, nurseries were very different from those of today. The big expansion of nurseries during the 1980s and 90s led to more options for working parents to consider nursery places for babies and children under the age of 3. This wider participation and the tighter government regulation that accompanied it prompted the development of curriculum frameworks and updated training programmes to guide the direction of early years practice and pedagogy. Nursery practitioners today are very familiar with the regular updating of early years policy and guidance on practice, including the time and energy that it takes to adjust to any change.

It is through discussion and the sharing of observations and ideas that we are enabled to think more carefully and with more curiosity about what children are experiencing. Elinor Goldschmied and Sonia Jackson's 1994 publication of *People Under Three: Young Children in Day Care* drew on Juliet Hopkins's findings to open up a wider early years sector conversation about the importance of listening to children and paying attention to their emotional needs. They introduced the term 'Key Person' to emphasise the importance for each child attending nursery and their families to have a special relationship with a named practitioner. The practical suggestions and strategies they offered on how to implement more emotionally attuned practice and why it was so important to do so were influential at that time and ultimately led to the statutory EYFS requirement that we have today for each child to have a Key Person (DfE, 2021).

Despite the significant changes that have taken place in nursery practice since the 1980s, it is interesting to note that examples of issues that were presented during the Froebel Trust funded practitioner Work Discussion group (Elfer *et al.*, 2018), introduced in Chapter 3, continue to include the complexity of professional attachment relationships. The majority of the issues that emerged from an analysis of the weekly discussions were concerns about children's development, but looking at the content more closely:

> These issues fell into two broad groups, one to do with children separating from the family member who had brought them to nursery and settling into the nursery or the degree of a child's attachment to a particular practitioner; the other was to do with managing behavioural boundaries and working with children on the autistic spectrum.
>
> (Elfer *et al.*, 2018, p. 13)

These practitioners embraced their work responsibilities and the challenges they experienced. They fully understood the expectations of the nursery to build close relationships with their key children and families and respond sensitively to their needs. But the emergence of these topics for discussion suggests that responding to the developmental needs of each child will always include dilemmas that need to be looked at afresh. With reference to attachment relationships, despite the guidance on the role of the Key Person and the systems in place in nurseries to ease children's transitions, each child's emotional response to separating from a family member and the process of developing a close relationship with their Key Person continues to evoke strong feelings for all involved. Each unique child brings with them their own experience of family relationships and different cultural practices, and each new professional attachment relationship with a child brings with it new insights and a range of expected and unexpected feelings. In Part Three of the book, more detailed examples of similar experiences are explored by the five Nursery Leaders.

In addition to the issues that we have looked at so far that focus on Work Discussion groups with practitioners working directly with children, research on themes brought to Work Discussion groups for nursery managers by Elfer (2012) and from the Froebel Trust funded evaluation of Work Discussion (Elfer *et al.*, 2018; Elfer and Wilson, 2021) illustrate that the content of the managers' discussions reflects their

Table 2.2 Themes discussed by the nursery managers in their Work Discussion group.

Themes discussed by the nursery managers
- The emotional toll of providing support for staff who were experiencing difficult personal situations or managing relationships when staff were not behaving professionally at work.
- The pressure of remaining professionally positive at all times despite difficult situations and circumstances.
- The loneliness of being in a position of responsibility for running a nursery without any system of support.
- Struggling meeting all the regulations and guidance as well as the financial responsibilities as a nursery provider in a market system.

leadership and management roles. The issues that managers and practitioners have shared, alongside the joys and satisfactions of these close relationships with children and maintaining relationships with families, nevertheless included a wide range of challenges and concerns (Elfer, 2012; Elfer and Wilson, 2021; Page and Elfer, 2013; Elfer and Page, 2015; Brace, 2021). These are summarised in Table 2.2:

The issues raised by these managers and practitioners illustrate the weight of their responsibilities and the need that they had for a forum where they were able to explore the challenges and dilemmas that they faced in their work roles. The more recent Froebel Trust funded nursery managers' Work Discussion group also chose to explore issues relating to the specific early years policy context within which they were working and the pressures that they experienced. In a similar way, they used the Work Discussion group to express their feelings and frustrations about the many external issues that they felt got in the way of focusing on the needs of the children and families they felt responsible for.

These findings show that opportunities for professional reflection are desperately needed for nursery practitioners and nursery leaders to acknowledge how they feel about their work and to discuss these feelings so that they impinge less on their direct work with children and families and instead, strengthen and deepen that work. The examples of the real daily dilemmas that practitioners and managers bring to Work Discussion illustrate the value of a forum where time can be given to listening to and teasing out the emotions that lie beneath the surface of professional practice in nurseries.

Note

1 The Tavistock Centre is based in North-West London, and one of its important functions is as a national training centre for professionals concerned with mental health, including teachers and nursery nurses.

PART TWO
Does Work Discussion work? A research evaluation from the perspectives of children, practitioners, and parents

Introducing the Froebel trust funded evaluation of Work Discussion

Peter Elfer

Members of the Early Childhood Teaching and Research Group at the University of Roehampton have been using Work Discussion with groups of nursery leaders and practitioners in many different parts of England over a good ten years. These groups were led by pairs of facilitators, one person who had worked with or in nurseries and one person with Work Discussion facilitation skills. By 2015, we had run around 20 programmes of Work Discussion in both the maintained and independent sectors.

Despite all this experience, we had never had the chance to formally research the possible effectiveness of Work Discussion. We had always asked for feedback from Work Discussion participants using evaluation forms. This kind of feedback is very helpful, but it does not usually count as reliable evidence of the effectiveness of a model of practice in nurseries. This is because the participants, through the evaluation forms, are telling the people who have run the programme what they think about the programme. It is easy to see that many participants may not want to say directly to the organisers what they really think, especially if it is not very positive!

We were thrilled as a team, therefore, in 2016, to be awarded a major research grant from the Froebel Trust. The grant was to evaluate Work Discussion in an outer London Authority with two groups of nursery practitioners. The first group was made up of the Head and some nursery practitioners from a large maintained nursery in that borough. This group met weekly for a year, ten times each term, resulting in 30 sessions from January to December 2017. The second group was for nursery managers of private nurseries in the same borough. This group met every two weeks for the same year. The evaluation funded by the Froebel Trust focussed mainly on the first group, as that was a much more frequent use of Work Discussion.

In our application to the Froebel Trust for the research grant, we had been very careful to specify that the team facilitating the Work Discussion groups would be kept completely separate from the team undertaking the research. For example, Antonia Zachariou, the researcher who interviewed the participants in both groups, assured each of them that what they told her about their experience of the groups would not be passed back to the people running the groups, in any way which might enable them to be identified.

Similarly, Sue Robson, who managed the evaluation of the children's progress during the year the Work Discussion group ran (essentially investigating whether or not Work Discussion made any difference to the children's progress), did so without sharing any of her observations with the people running the Work Discussion groups.

Finally, Sue Greenfield, the researcher who interviewed parents of children attending the nursery centre, also reassured the parents that whatever they said to her would not be shared with practitioners in the nursery or those running the WD groups.

In addition, Antonia, Sue, and Sue did not engage in any discussions about the WD sessions themselves with the people running them.

In this way, we hoped that any findings about the value of WD would be seen as both trustworthy and objective.

As an overall team (the Work Discussion facilitators team and the research evaluation team), we are hugely grateful to the Trust for providing the research funding. The Trust always receives more applications for grants than it has money to fund. Selection processes are rigorous, but there is always an element of judgement involved about what may make the most difference, in the short and long term, to the wellbeing of children and their families. We are very grateful to the Trust for their confidence in the project.

In the next chapter, Chapter 4, Antonia Zachariou tells us what the practitioners in the Work Discussion groups really thought about the sessions and whether they felt the groups helped their work as pedagogues or not.

Sue Robson then follows in Chapter 5, analysing and discussing her findings on the progress the children made during the year that Work Discussion was going on. She addresses the question of whether or not it can be said that Work Discussion makes a positive difference for children's learning and progress.

Finally, in Chapter 6, Sue Greenfield describes her interviews with parents. All three chapters offer some interesting – and surprising – results. We hope you enjoy what these three researchers found, as well as learning something from the way these researchers undertook their separate tasks.

4 Does Work Discussion 'work'? What did the practitioners think about their Work Discussion group experience?

Antonia Zachariou

In this chapter, we look at the following:

▉ How we collected practitioners views on Work Discussion.

▉ What the practitioners' dispositions and expectations were about the Work Discussion sessions before these started.

▉ Practitioners' evaluation of their experience of the Work Discussion group discussions.

▉ Practitioners' views on the benefits and drawbacks of the Work Discussion groups.

Introduction: How did we collect practitioners' views?

This chapter looks at the perspectives of the practitioners who participated in the 'Work Discussion' project for a year. The Work Discussion sessions happened at the end of the nursery working day. Did the practitioners think it was helpful and worthwhile staying at the end of the day to sit, talk and think together about their work? Or would they have preferred to go home earlier?

To find out what practitioners thought about Work Discussion, and how they evaluated their experiences, I (an independent researcher who had no involvement in the Work Discussions) interviewed the participating practitioners. From the beginning to the end of the project, 14 practitioners in total were interviewed. The one-to-one interviews with practitioners were conducted at three times throughout the year: once at the start, once midway through and once at the end of the year. All practitioners were asked similar questions, so in the results later, each result is reported and compared with the total of 14 participants.

DOI: 10.4324/b23247-6

In this chapter, we look at how practitioners felt about engaging in the Work Discussion sessions before these started. Then we look at how they evaluated their experience of Work Discussion groups and whether or not they thought that there were any benefits and drawbacks in participating in Work Discussion groups. In so doing, we identify aspects that are useful for consideration by others considering implementing Work Discussion.

How did the practitioners' feel about the Work Discussion sessions, and what did they expect before these started?

Before the start of the group, practitioners were mostly negative about the idea of participating. They were worried about the time commitment involved, the length of the sessions and having to stay at work late, although they were compensated for this additional time by being able to finish work earlier on another day in the week. As Marina put it: 'We have so many things to do . . . So at first (I thought) here is another thing to do' (Marina).

A few practitioners were also nervous about having to speak in front of other people. As practitioners explained, they were not confident about speaking in large groups or in front of people they did not know:

> I was a bit nervous because I did not know what it was. I was shy as well, because it was a bigger group . . . It was my team members but it was also two people from outside.
>
> (Beena)

At the same time, there were some positive attitudes expressed about the idea of participating in Work Discussion groups. Three of the practitioners expressed their interest in and positive attitude towards these Work Discussion groups (Gabriel, Alice, Salma). Alice, who joined in later than the core of the groups, explained how she felt the first time she heard about these groups: 'they were telling me about it and I said "oh that sounds quite nice", because I didn't have it in my old place'.

Practitioners' evaluation of their experience of the Work Discussion group discussions

In this section, we look at how practitioners evaluated Work Discussion in terms of two elements. First, we look at what they thought regarding *the process and structure* of the Work Discussion groups and then we look at how they felt about *the content* of Work Discussion groups.

How did the practitioners evaluate the process and structure of the Work Discussion groups?

We asked the practitioners to discuss what went well in terms of process and structure and what did not go well.

Most of the practitioners spoke positively about how the Work Discussion groups worked well, ran well and had a nice flow. The practitioners appeared to appreciate a change that happened from Phase 2 onwards. According to practitioners, this change helped the meetings to flow much better and helped avoid the many awkward silences in the early sessions. In Aziza's words:

> Previously when you started (the Work Discussion group) you would go straight into talking about your children, and it was very awkward. . . . The facilitators picked up on that and we discussed what we can do. We suggested maybe talking about other things first, to break the ice. So now we start by discussing how our week has been and it is a bit more relaxed. That's quite nice.
>
> (Aziza)

What did the facilitators of Work Discussion groups do, in terms of structure, that worked well?

The approach of the facilitators (the two people leading) of the Work Discussion group was mostly discussed in a positive light. For the practitioners, the following were important:

- the facilitators appreciated and respected their time;

- in terms of the process and the structure, the practitioners also appreciated that the facilitators would encourage them to speak and discuss and would listen to and value all input; and

- practitioners greatly appreciated that the facilitators would never put pressure on specific people to speak.

There were two elements that according to the practitioners did not work well. The first element, that almost all practitioners mentioned, had to do with the facilitators' expectation that the practitioners would bring a written observation to the Work Discussion group if it was their turn to present. However, all the practitioners explained that they did not feel they had enough time to write an observation. At the same time, most of the practitioners also acknowledged that, when either they or another practitioner brought notes to the Work Discussion group, this appeared to help in the presentation of whatever it was the practitioner wanted to talk about. As one of the practitioners, who had made some notes rather than bringing a full observation, explained: 'thinking that you only need to write notes rather than a case study makes it more relaxed, less stressful and more likely to do' (Gabriel). Thus, maybe this could be the way forward for future Work Discussion groups. The second element that was a problem had to do with people's hesitation to talk, which led to either awkward silences or to some people doing more talking than others. A lot of the practitioners hinted that they felt uncomfortable on those occasions when nobody responded to a question.

How did the practitioners evaluate what was talked about in the Work Discussion groups?

The practitioners found the content of the Work Discussion groups important, often saying that they enjoyed the meetings. They thought the facilitators asked interesting, thought-provoking questions, and they valued the facilitators' expressions of admiration for their work.

About a third of the participants expected more from the facilitators in the form of advice and with less focus on exploring presented issues, which they sometimes found uncomfortable. Some practitioners expressed this dissatisfaction by describing a feeling of 'digging too deep'.

> I remember these like therapy. It's always about how do we feel about . . . , don't we get annoyed . . . in our practice if a child does something. Sometimes all these questions have that feeling of therapy. . . . Actually, I don't feel like this (annoyed), because it is my job and I try to understand my children.
>
> (Marina)

Most, however, said they experienced the groups as generally comfortable, and three spoke of how these groups allowed them to open up emotionally, see things that they felt they already knew more clearly and deal better with their feelings so that they could focus on their work more effectively.

Practitioners' views on the drawbacks and benefits of the Work Discussion groups

Drawbacks of Work Discussion groups

The major drawback of the Work Discussion groups identified was having to stay at the setting after work. Practitioners' concern regarding time was more prominent in the first term than in the second or third terms. Of all the practitioners who participated, almost all had clearly stated that they were not happy with staying longer at the setting. An example of this feeling came from Hayley: 'You just want to go home at 4:30, isn't it? Because you have had a really long day on Monday, you just want to go home'. She also, understandably, mentioned childcare issues for her own children, if she had to stay longer at work. About a third of the practitioners also said that the length of the Work Discussion sessions could have been shorter.

Another significant drawback that emerged was that sometimes they felt that their points were misinterpreted during the groups, that they were not understood. As Aziza explained, 'Sometimes there can be a lot of misunderstandings that come up'. Given that these feelings could have potentially had negative effects on the practitioners' practice, in terms of levels of stress and satisfaction in practitioners' work, it could be important for Work Discussion facilitators to ensure that time is given for participants to raise the issue if they think there has been a misunderstanding and to clarify any misunderstandings.

Benefits of the Work Discussion groups

All the participants thought the Work Discussion groups had benefits in their work with children and families. Perceptions of the kinds of benefits varied but included practitioners being less judgemental, more understanding, better able to empathise, better sharing of information within the team and thinking more deeply and more objectively about the children.

Change in the relationships with children and parents

The practitioners described that the Work Discussion groups had an effect on their relationships with parents and children. Regarding their relationships with children, the practitioners reported that they felt they had grown closer with the child they discussed in the Work Discussion groups. Stella talked about her bond with one of her key children, who was discussed at the Work Discussion groups: 'His relationship with me is much closer. . . . Apparently he always talks about me at home. . . . Our relationship is much better'. This impact of the Work Discussion groups on the practitioners' interactions with children is looked at in more depth later.

Most of the practitioners also thought that the Work Discussion groups helped them change their relationships with parents for the better. They explained this by saying that now they felt that they were less judgemental, more understanding towards the parents and more able to empathise. Some of them put this down to having a better appreciation of what the parents were going through because of all the discussions which were held during the Work Discussion groups.

> ### An example of Work Discussion helping change the relationship with a child's parent
>
> Salma gave an example of how she was in the process of changing her relationship with a parent:
>
>> From my point of view, mum . . . was not fully engaging and fully wishing to help us (settle in her child). . . . But the way we spoke about this case in the group discussion, it helped me to see her from a different point of view and say 'maybe I was too critical. . . . Maybe I should try a different way of approaching her'. . . . So I am not being as critical towards her as I was before that discussion.
>
> Salma then went on to explain:
>
>> My thinking about how I want to next approach this mum has changed. (Parents had been unwell and the child was not attending, so maybe we could) Get them a get-well card and tell them that we are still thinking about them and we are waiting for them to come back. To encourage them. Just to know that we have not forgotten them.

Changes in the relationship with other practitioners

Most of the practitioners talked about how they felt the Work Discussion groups had brought some changes in their relationship with other practitioners. For them, the Work Discussion groups brought the team closer. Aziza, for example, talked about this:

> I think it has brought everybody closer, because it is the one time when we can actually talk to each other. . . . Very rarely are we all *together* because our schedules are so busy every day of the week'. She then went on to add that 'It's brought everybody closer, I know it has. I can just see the difference. As soon as this started, it just made everybody come together, with everything that was happening with the team losing staff.

Impact on practitioners' feelings

It was most interesting to see that most of the practitioners acknowledged the Work Discussion groups as being linked to their feelings. At a first level, practitioners acknowledged how this was a comfortable and open discussion group, where it was 'ok to say how you feel'. In this way, they were acknowledging that talking about feelings was acceptable in the Work Discussion group environment.

Some practitioners went a step further and explained that for them, these groups were cathartic. As Gabriel said, 'I really enjoy doing the groups. Even at the bottom level, it is quite cathartic being able to talk about your children after the session and talking about things that went well, things that didn't'. Some of the practitioners drew parallels between Work Discussion groups and group therapy and explained how these groups made them feel stronger.

At an even deeper level of reflection, three of the practitioners spoke of how these groups allowed them to open up emotionally and see more clearly things that they already knew. Aziza's words indicate deep thinking and awareness of this:

> it (the Work Discussion group) just helped me clear my mind. I knew that stuff (already), but it was like my vision was blurred. . . . I knew the history of that child, but talking through it, it opened me up a bit emotionally . . . and then to talk through it and have all these questions, it did make a huge difference.

An example of the impact of Work Discussion groups on practitioners' feelings

Alexandra's comment in the next section clearly illustrates how the Work Discussion groups had an effect on practitioner's feelings and how they offered a place where practitioners could talk about their feelings and deal with them so that then they could focus on their work:

> For me it's almost like a kettle. So you boil the kettle, stuff comes up, which is your stuff, and then it cools down and then you are able to deal with your work effectively . . . with the families that you are working with.
>
> As an organisation, when your staff are dealing with challenging families, you have to find a way of allowing them to express their feelings so that they are able to be effective for your organisation. And this, I thought, was amazing.

Perceived impact on their practice

When prompted to consider whether or not the Work Discussion groups had any impact on their work, it was interesting to note varied responses,

Depth in thinking affects how practitioners approach children

A lot of the ways in which Work Discussion groups influenced practitioners' work came down to the element of depth. They often mentioned that the depth of information they learnt about a child through the Work Discussion groups and the depth of thinking that was promoted in the Work Discussion groups had an effect on their practice.

According to almost all of the practitioners, the Work Discussion groups brought to light background and deeper information about children. For the practitioners, it was important that all the team was now aware of this information and they explained how this information helped them in understanding the parent and the child's behaviours. Gabriel gives an example of how this took place:

> I had no idea about this child's background. . . . We thought that the parent was really over protective of that child. But then with some of the information that came up during the discussion it was completely obvious why and I didn't know any of that background. But then, again, I think it made me understand some of the parent's behaviours but also some of the child's behaviours.

In addition to this, most of the practitioners also linked these Work Discussion groups with thinking more deeply and looking at the children more closely and deeply. More specifically, the practitioners felt that they would now become more aware and be keen to explore alternative reasons why something was happening. They often explained how they would now try to look for the underlying causes of children's behaviours. Daria explained that they would discuss a particular child in the session but that then they also thought about other children, adopting the same idea of going into depth: 'You think about why other children are doing particular things or sometimes we just think a bit more deep on why the child is reacting like that. It could be because at home there could be something going on'.

As a result of knowing more about the children and of thinking more deeply about the underlying causes of children's behaviours, a lot of the practitioners reported that they would now approach the children differently. The practitioners explained that they would address behaviours differently, often in a less firm way than they would have done in the past. Marina gave an example:

> there are challenging children and at first you would say 'oh God he is doing this again'. But then you find out . . . what is behind the behaviour, you . . . see it differently. You (try to) keep calm and try to explain again and again if you have to or try different things.

An example of how thinking deeply about the children changed the practitioners' practice for the better

Gabriel gave an example of approaching children in a less firm way, different from what they would normally do, and how this seemed to work best for the child's needs:

> Not even consciously, but I just felt myself interacting with this child differently after that (Work Discussion group). In the past (I would deal with this in) a firmer and

really immediate (way). But after talking about it . . . it would be (me) taking the child away to another activity and spending more one-to-one time with them and seeing a kind of improvement . . . because it stopped tantrums after the problem behaviour and it gave the child more one-to-one attention, which was what he needed.

The practitioners think more and think more objectively before they act

Some of the practitioners also explained how they would now always think more before they acted. As Zena said, this has made her 'More self-aware. Having more thought before doing something'. In addition to this, some of the practitioners explained how they were now able to take a step back and think more objectively about the child's behaviour because the unbiased or different perspectives on the children and the situations from others in the Work Discussion groups encouraged them to do so. Paloma talked about how she would transfer the attitude of taking a step back and thinking about the situation, which she learnt in the case studies discussed at the Work Discussion groups, to similar cases with the children in her own key group:

So something similar or something completely different happens and then you try to think of another way of looking at the situation, so it broadens your mind a little bit, rather than having a preconceived idea about why things are happening.

More practical issues

In terms of more practical issues, the practitioners emphasised that through these Work Discussion groups, they learnt from finding out how the rest of team would engage with the children. This, according to them, played a key role in improving their practice. As Christine explained:

maybe then it (Work Discussion groups) might channel some other ideas that you could get and see if there is something that (the other practitioners) might think and they might say 'why don't you try it like that', because they have experienced it before. . . . In other words, if somebody tells you 'maybe try that'. It is not seen as a negative thing. It is a positive thing. You are all learning from each other anyway all the time.

The practitioners also clearly talked about the Work Discussion groups becoming an incentive for changes in their practice. Stella, from her first interview, explained how this would take place:

Sometimes I will think: maybe we could do this or do that and maybe the next day we will discuss it together. . . . Let's see from what was discussed, let's see if we can help in some way.

Impact on children's outcomes

We look more closely at the children's outcomes in the next chapter, but it is interesting here to see some of the practitioners discussing how they thought that the Work Discussion groups had an impact on children's progress. Even though they widely acknowledged that it was very difficult to separate the effects of Work Discussion groups from the children's maturation or other effects, they were able to give examples of children where they thought that Work Discussion groups had a clear impact on the children's outcomes. For each child, practitioners seemed to pinpoint the area where the child was facing most challenges as the area where the child's outcomes improved. For some children, this had to do with accelerated social and emotional development, for another child, this had to do with being happier at the nursery and for another case, this had to do with physical development. An example of accelerated social and emotional development comes from Gabriel's interview: 'There might be a couple of children where their social and emotional development . . . has probably developed a bit quicker since we started doing those Work Discussion groups, because we are approaching them in a different way'. As the practitioner noted, it was the change in the way the practitioners would approach the children that seemed to mainly affect the children's outcomes. Gabriel continued his thinking by giving the following example:

> One child, if I ask him to stop doing something, he will look very upset, because he doesn't like to make the adult angry. But my approach now is a little bit different with him, because I try to approach him in a way that he will not experience that feeling that he has made someone that he cares about upset. So, I try to do it in a more playful way . . . rather than saying 'stop'. . . . So (in this way) he can deal with the problem of having to stop playing and do what he wants to do . . . without those feelings of guilt and sadness. (I am doing this) To help him understand that things can be delayed and it is fine to stop one thing and do something else.

The route via which the children's outcomes changed was always linked to the practitioners' approach which was informed by the Work Discussion groups. Different practitioners cited different changes in their approach, such as being calmer or more positive. Also, two of the practitioners maintained that for some children, their outcomes improved mainly because the whole team was now aware of their challenges and everybody now approached the child in the same way. This consistency in practitioners' approach had a beneficial effect on the children's outcomes.

Practitioners also thought that the Work Discussion had an effect on other children and not just the children discussed in the Work Discussion groups. Salma's thoughts later explain how the Work Discussion groups had an impact on a lot of the children's outcomes through a change in the practitioners' approach. According to her, if the practitioners are positive with the children (because of the Work

Discussion groups), the children will also be more receptive and have a more positive attitude:

> They will learn different things because the way we ask questions, the way we praise them, the way we deal with them . . . have a positive or negative impact on children. For me, analysing (in the Work Discussion groups) will definitely have a positive impact on the children's learning and attitude. Children can really feel what you feel and respond in different ways (attuned) to the way you respond to them. So if you are very positive towards them, they will give the same attitude to you.

Practitioners' views on the benefits of Work Discussion for their professional development

Around half the participants explicitly said that the groups had improved their longer-term professional development, including an increase in confidence and in curiosity about theory, together with nurturing their ability to reflect, think deeply and look for reasons behind children's and parents' behaviours. The other half of the participants were uncertain about the impact of the sessions on their professional development. However, all of them, at other points in their interviews, mentioned skills or knowledge they had acquired that were closely linked to their professional development. This suggests that the practitioners' understanding of the Work Discussion groups' impact on their professional development was still implicit and that we potentially need to allow practitioners' time to process their learning and understanding before we ask them to evaluate it.

Conclusion

In this chapter, we have looked at practitioners' perspectives about their Work Discussion group experience. We interviewed all practitioners who participated in Work Discussion.

What we found was that before participating, practitioners initially had negative dispositions about engaging in Work Discussion. However, later, in evaluating their experiences, they spoke positively about how the Work Discussion groups worked well, ran well and had a nice flow. They also appreciated the encouragement and appreciation and respect they felt from the facilitators and the thought-provoking questions that they asked. At the same time, they explained that they encountered two difficulties: lack of time meant that it was not possible for them to prepare a case study for a child before their Work Discussion group, and they found silences in the discussions 'awkward'.

As a significant drawback, they mentioned the time the groups took, but as benefits, they described positive changes in their relationships with children, parents and practitioners and a cathartic impact on their own feelings. Practitioners also described how these Work Discussion groups had an impact on their practice: they believed that would now think more deeply about the children and approach them differently, and they would think more and more objectively before they act, with this having direct implications for their professional development. Finally, they speculated that Work Discussion might have been the reason for a positive change they were seeing in children's outcomes.

5 Does Work Discussion 'work'?

Is it beneficial for the children?

Sue Robson

In this chapter, we look at the following:

- The importance of looking at the potential impact of Work Discussion on the children.
- How we decided what to look for.
- The Child Observation Framework we developed and how it links to the EYFS and other practice and curriculum guidance.
- The progress the children made.
- Whether Work Discussion may be especially beneficial for particular children or not.

Introduction: the importance of children's personal, social and emotional development

We looked in Chapter 4 at what practitioners said about their involvement in Work Discussion. In this chapter, we look at what must surely be a central reason for engaging in Work Discussion: the potential benefits for the children involved.

How did we set about trying to find this out, and how could we know if it did? We turned first to the requirements for young children in England, the location for our research. This is the *Statutory Framework for the Early Years Foundation Stage* (Department for Education, 2021a). This document identifies seven areas of learning and development. Of these, three are seen as 'prime'. One of these perhaps underpins all others, that is, the area of personal, social and emotional development, described in the following way:

> Children's personal, social and emotional development (PSED) is crucial for children to lead healthy and happy lives, and is fundamental to their

DOI: 10.4324/b23247-7

cognitive development. Underpinning their personal development are the important attachments that shape their social world. Strong, warm and supportive relationships with adults enable children to learn how to understand their own feelings and those of others.

(Department for Education, 2021a, pp. 8–9)

Our starting point, then, was to look at the effect of the practitioners' involvement in WD on the children's PSED, both for its own sake and also because of its importance for aspects such as their cognitive development.

A framework for observing children's development

The use of observation to support practitioners' knowledge and understanding, planning, assessment and reporting has a long history in early childhood. Its importance is recognised in the Foundation Stage Profile for England, which says that 'Teachers' judgements will largely be based on whether or not children are learning what has been taught and from their observations of development during day-to-day activity in the classroom' (Department for Education, 2021b, p. 8). For this study, it had multiple advantages. As Azevedo (2009) identifies, observations (1) record what children actually do, (2) afford links between behaviour and context, (3) do not depend on verbal abilities, (4) allow for recording of verbal and non-verbal behaviours (including aspects such as eye gaze) and (5) allow for recording of social processes.

We began by developing a Child Observation Framework (COF) to guide our observations. Reflecting the version of the EYFS in operation at the time that the project was carried out, we drew on the PSED section of *Development Matters in the Early Years Foundation Stage* (Early Education, 2012), written to provide practitioner guidance in implementing the EYFS. This included using their overlapping age bands to identify the children's progress. The children in our study ranged in age from 29 months to 37 months at the start of the project. However, the setting is located in an area of multiple disadvantages, and many of the children had also been referred there because of concerns about their development, so we included four of the overlapping age bands from *Development Matters*, starting from younger than the children's chronological ages: 8–20 months, 16–26 months, 22–36 months and 30–50 months.

Drawing on the organisation of the EYFS in operation at the time, the Child Observation Framework comprises three categories: *Making Relationships, Self-Confidence and Self-Awareness and Managing Feelings and Behaviour*. We have included a copy at the end of the chapter to give an idea of what we were looking for.

Looking at personal, social and emotional development across the early years

When this study was conducted, we used the guidance in *Development Matters in the Early Years* (Early Education, 2012) to construct the COF. Throughout this chapter, we use these descriptors, but in order to reflect the latest guidance, we have also included examples of comparable statements from both *Birth to 5 Matters* (Early Years Coalition, 2021) and *Development Matters* (Department for Education, 2021c). So for example, later, we show how items from the 'Making Relationships' category in the COF can be mapped onto equivalent statements from *Birth to 5 Matters* and *Development Matters*.

Making Relationships

Child Observation Framework	Birth to 5 Matters (2021)	Development Matters (2021c)
(Organised in four overlapping age bands.)	(Organised in six age ranges. Four apply here: ranges 2–5.)	(Organised in three age ranges. Two apply here: birth to 3 and 3- and 4-year-olds.)
<u>Ages 8–20 months</u> • Seeks to gain attention, drawing others into interaction. • Builds relationships with special people. • Wary of unfamiliar people.	<u>Range 2 (approx. 12–18 months)</u> • Draws others into social interaction through calling, crying and babbling, smiling, laughing and moving their bodies and limbs. • Builds relationships with special people. • Is wary of unfamiliar people.	<u>Birth to 3</u> • Engage with others through gestures, gaze and talk.
<u>Ages 16–26 months</u> • Plays alongside others. • Uses familiar adult as secure base to explore independently in new environments.	<u>Range 3 (approx. 18–24 months)</u> • Enjoys playing alone and alongside others and is also interested in being together and playing with other children. • Explores the environment, interacts with others and plays confidently, while their parent/carer or Key Person is close by, using them as a secure base to return to for reassurance if anxious or in unfamiliar situations.	<u>Birth to 3</u> • Play with increasing confidence on their own and with other children because they know their Key Person is nearby and available.

Ages 22–36 months	Range 4 (approx. 24–36 months)	Birth to 3
• Seeks out others to share experiences. • May form special friendship with another child.	• Seeks out others to share experiences with and may choose to play with a familiar friend or a child who has similar interest.	• Develop friendships with other children.
Ages 30–50 months	Range 5 (approx. 36–48 months)	3- to 4-year-olds
• Can play in a group, extending and elaborating play ideas. • Initiates play, offering cues to peers to join. • Keeps play going by responding to what others are saying or doing.	• Seeks out companionship with adults and other children, sharing experiences and play ideas. • Enjoys playing alone, alongside and with others, inviting others to play and attempting to join others' play.	• Play with one or more other children, extending and elaborating play ideas.

What did we do to try to find out?

At three different points over a period of six months, we collected 444 video recordings of 23 children (eight boys, 15 girls, which reflected the gender balance of the groups). As we have seen in earlier chapters, not all practitioners will choose to participate in Work Discussion, and not all children get to be discussed in a Work Discussion session. So looking at our 23 children, eight of them had a Key Person who participated, seven were the subject of a Work Discussion (and thus, their Key Person participated too) and eight had a Key Person who did not participate. The observations were made in all areas of the nursery, indoors and out, and included children playing alone, with others and with or without an adult being present. I recorded snack times, large-group activities and small-group times of children with their Key Person. I did not record children in contexts such as self-care or nappy changes, feeling that to be overly intrusive.

The recordings were made by myself, as a researcher, as I noticed activities and also ensuring that I observed as wide a range of activities as possible. They often included instances of children themselves asking to be recorded, either verbally or, for example, taking me by the hand or bringing things to show to the video camera. The children also asked to look through it and to watch themselves on the recordings. They were used to being photographed during their everyday activities and rapidly became comfortable with the video camera (often more so than the adults!). Importantly, I did not make recordings without children's knowledge and always tried to ensure that they gave their consent for us to record them. I also stopped whenever a child indicated that they did not want to be recorded, either verbally or through a gesture, such as pushing the adult or the camera away. It is also important to note that all of the children's names here are pseudonyms.

The first set of recordings was made before the WD sessions began to give us a picture of the children at the outset. We made a second set after three months and a final set after six months. We then undertook the task of coding what happened in all 444 observations, ascribing behaviour according to the descriptors and age bands set out in the Child Observation Framework. The next box has examples of what that coding looks like in practice, with examples of children in the category 'Managing Feelings and Behaviour'.

Managing Feelings and Behaviour

The three extracts here show examples of children's behaviour in the category 'Managing Feelings and Behaviour', with the relevant Child Observation Framework items next to them (see full Framework at end of chapter).

Zahira (29 months) is at the snack table, sitting opposite practitioner M. She has a chunk of banana and a knife and manages to cut through the banana.

Zahira (to M): 'I did it! Look! I did it!' (smiling).

Zahira: band 8–20 months, 'Uses familiar adult to share feelings such as excitement or pleasure and for "emotional refuelling" when tired, stressed or frustrated'.

Sabira (33 months) sees Saadiqa (31 months) fall over outside and start to cry. She runs over to a box of tissues on the windowsill and takes one to her.

Sabira: band 22–36 months, 'Tries to help or comfort when others are distressed'.

Ifran (35 months) and Milo (29 months) are outside looking at a wall display of photographs of a trip to the park. Milo has binoculars around his neck but is not looking through them. Ifran reaches across to look through them, but Milo holds onto them and puts them up to his eyes, looking through them. Ifran stands next to him, waiting.

Ifran: band 30–50 months, 'Begins to accept the needs of others, can take turns and share' and 'Tolerates delay when needs not immediately met'.

They go over to a balancing plank. Milo goes to walk along it, still using the binoculars, but he dislodges the plank. Ifran moves the plank back into position.

Ifran: 'There you go' (stands back and smiles at Milo).

Milo walks to the end and then gives Ifran the binoculars. Ifran smiles.

What did we find out? Did the children make better progress than we might have expected?

The study lasted for six months, so we could expect some changes in the children's PSED over that time. However, were the changes better than we might expect as a result of them being six months older?

At the start of the study, the children's ages ranged from 29 to 37 months. The results from the first set of recordings, made before Work Discussion began, showed that the PSED of the great majority of the children fell below their chronological age. Eight of the children displayed most behaviour in the band 8–20 months, 14 evidenced most behaviour in the band 16–26 months and one child was in the 30–50 months band, matching his chronological age of 35 months

Over the course of six months, 21 of the 23 children made progress. One boy was already at the highest age band (30–50 months), and a second boy stayed at the same overall level. For a further six children, the progress they made was age-appropriate, marked by gains of about 6–8 months. However, the gains made by the remaining 14 were significantly better and ranged between 15 and 26 months. So overall, nearly two thirds of the children made PSED gains that went well beyond what could be expected as a result of them being six months older.

So much for the statistics. What does this look like in practice for the children? Let's look at extracts from three observations of Afia and some of the evidence for her in the category 'Making Relationships'.

Afia: Making Relationships

The three extracts here show the progress Afia (30 months at start) made. At the beginning of the study, most of the evidence we collected about Afia was below her chronological age, with only a quarter at roughly her chronological age. By the end of it, this had more than doubled, and the majority of evidence we collected was either at or above her chronological age.

January

Afia (30 months) takes her coat off peg and starts to put it on, putting her right arm in the left arm of the coat. She continues trying, then takes it off and lets it dangle from her arm. She spots practitioner E and walks over to her, but E is talking to another child and walks away. Afia turns and follows E right around the room. She stops and stands behind E, who is talking to another child.

Band 8–20 months, 'Seeks to gain attention, drawing others into interaction'.

<u>March</u>

Afia (32 months) is in the water tray, filling a cylinder. Sabira puts a ball in the top of the cylinder, and Afia gestures to her to remove it.	Band 8–20 months, 'Interacts with others'.
Practitioner E crouches down next to Afia, who holds out her bottle to show her.	Band 16–26 months, 'Plays cooperatively with familiar adult'.
Practitioner E (to Afia): 'What have you got there?'	
Afia shows her the bottle is filled with water, then pours it into the cylinder.	

<u>July</u>

Outside, Joseph is 'grabbing' at Milo with a large plastic sand toy with hinged scoops. Afia (36 months) watches from several metres away, finger in mouth. She walks over, smiles and holds out her hands to Joseph. Milo takes the toy, and the boys start to walk away. Afia follows and joins them.	Band 22–36 months, 'Interested in others' play And starting to join in'.

For a number of other children, the gains were even more dramatic, as we shall see with Noah next.

Was Work Discussion more beneficial for some children than others?

Perhaps the most important, and encouraging, point to make here is that all groups of children made very real progress, beyond what might be expected – younger and older children, boys and girls, higher and lower attaining children. This means that WD may be valuable generally.

The amount of progress made by different children was well distributed across the three groups of (1) children whose Key Person participated, (2) children who were discussed in a Work Discussion session and (3) children whose KP did not participate. Interestingly, there was a small advantage to individual children if their Key Person participated, in comparison with the group as a whole, but children whose Key Person did not participate, or who were not discussed in a Work Discussion session, generally made as much progress as those who were. It is useful to look back at what the practitioners themselves said about Work Discussion. A number of those who participated talked about how their involvement in Work Discussion had an impact on their interactions and relationships with *all* of the children, not just those discussed or those for whom they were the Key Person. So practitioners' participation in Work Discussion may be potentially valuable for all children.

However, it is useful to look at the evidence about some specific children. In particular, those who, at the start, were assessed as having the lowest levels of

PSED. The effects of the practitioners' involvement in Work Discussion was often particularly positive for these children. Let's look at Noah. Noah's Key Person participated, and he was also himself a subject of discussion in a Work Discussion session. In the first round of observations, Noah's personal, social and emotional development was limited and consistently below his chronological age. By the end of the study, a majority of the evidence for Noah was either at or above his chronological age. The next examples show his developing competence and confidence.

Noah: Self-Confidence and Self-Awareness

The three extracts here are taken from observations of Noah over the course of six months, focusing on Self-Confidence and Self-Awareness. They show the significant progress he made. Initially, all of the evidence was below his chronological age, much of it in the 8–20 months band. By July, over 70 percent of his behaviour matched items in the 30–50 months band. The Child Observation Checklist items are shown here, along with comparable items from *Birth to 5 Matters* (2021) and *Development Matters* (2021c) for reference.

January

Noah (34 months) is on the carpet looking at a book. Practitioner R and Kara are nearby, looking at a book together. Noah shouts out, pointing at his book and looking towards R.

Child Observation Checklist, band 8–20 months: 'Uses pointing with eye gaze to make requests and share an interest'.

Birth to 5 Matters (2021) range 2, 12–18 months: 'Understands that their own voice and actions causes an effect on others'.

Development Matters (2021c) birth-to-3 section: 'Engage with others through gestures, gaze and talk'.

March

Noah (37 months) is at the snack table with practitioner V and other children. They see some children dancing in another part of the room.

Noah: 'Dancing!'

V: 'You can go and join them once you've finished, join in the dancing if you want to.'

Noah: 'No.'

Child Observation Checklist, band 16–26 months: 'Demonstrates sense of self as an individual, e.g. wants to do things independently, says 'No' to adult'.

Birth to 5 Matters (2021) range 3, 18–24 months: 'Shows their growing sense of self through asserting their likes and dislikes, choices, decisions, and ideas. These may be different to those of the adult or their peers; often saying no, me do it or mine'.

Development Matters (2021c) Birth-to-3 section: 'Express preferences and decisions. They also try new things and start establishing their autonomy'.

July	Child Observation Checklist, band 30–50 months: 'Enjoys responsibility of carrying out small tasks'.
Practitioner V is outdoors with several children. Noah (40 months) is nearby, holding a tennis bat.	
V (to Noah and two other boys): 'Can you help me? It's heavy' (picking up large block).	*Birth to 5 Matters* (2021) range 5, 36–48 months: 'Enjoys a sense of belonging through being involved in daily tasks'.
Noah (runs over, picks up the other end of the block and walks excitedly with V): 'Choo-choo!' (singing, carries it with her, putting it down in place next to a balancing circuit)	*Development Matters* (2021c) 3- and 4-year-olds section: 'Develop their sense of responsibility and membership of a community'.

Noah's developing confidence and awareness, both with regard to himself and to those around him, is clear. It is, then, worth bearing in mind that the benefits of Work Discussion may be particularly positively felt by those children with lower levels of PSED, with all that means for their overall development.

Conclusion

In this chapter, we have looked at why it is important to think about whether or not Work Discussion benefits the children. We have looked at the Child Observation Framework, developed for the project to support the observations we made, using PSED as a way of focusing our thinking.

What we found was that Work Discussion seems to have a positive impact on the personal, social and emotional development of many of the children, beyond what we could expect as a result of them just getting older during the lifetime of the project. This was true for all groups of children. At the same time, we also found that it may be particularly valuable for children who, at the outset, have lower levels of development in PSED than their peers. All of this highlights the possible advantages of Work Discussion and suggests that, for practitioners, it may be a valuable routine to try to include in their practice.

Child Observation Framework

Drawing on *Development Matters in the Early Years* (Early Education, 2012)

1 Making Relationships	Ages 8–20 months	1 Seeks to gain attention, drawing others into interaction. 2 Builds relationships with special people. 3 Wary of unfamiliar people. 4 Interacts with others, explores new situations supported by familiar person. 5 Shows interest in others' activities, responds to children and adults.
	Ages 16–26 months	6 Plays alongside others. 7 Uses familiar adult as secure base to explore independently in new environments. 8 Plays cooperatively with familiar adult.
	Ages 22–36 months	9 Interested in others' play and starting to join in. 10 Seeks out others to share experiences. 11 Shows affection and concern for people special to them. 12 May form special friendship with another child.
	Ages 30–50 months	13 Can play in a group, extending and elaborating play ideas. 14 Initiates play, offering cues to peers to join. 15 Keeps play going by responding to what others are saying or doing. 16 Demonstrates friendly behaviour, initiating conversation and forming good relationships with peers and familiar adults.
2 Self-Confidence Self-Awareness	Ages 8–20 months	1 Enjoys finding own nose, eyes or tummy as part of naming games. 2 Learns that own voice and actions have effects on others. 3 Uses pointing with eye gaze to make requests and to share an interest. 4 Engages other person to help achieve a goal.
	Ages 16–26 months	5 Explores new toys and environments. 'Checks in' with familiar adult as needed. 6 Engages in pretend play with toys. 7 Demonstrates sense of self as an individual (e.g. wants to do things independently, says 'No' to adult).
	Ages 22–36 months	8 Separates from main carer with support and encouragement from familiar adult. 9 Expresses own preferences and interests.

	Ages 30–50 months	10 Can select and use activities and resources with help.
		11 Welcomes and values praise for what has done.
		12 Enjoys responsibility of carrying out small tasks.
		13 Outgoing to unfamiliar people, confident in new social situations.
		14 Confident to talk to other children when playing.
		15 Shows confidence in asking adults for help.

3 Managing Feelings and Behaviour

Ages 8–20 months	1 Uses familiar adult to share feelings, such as excitement or pleasure, and for 'emotional refuelling' when feeling tired, stressed or frustrated.
	2 Growing ability to soothe themselves, may use a comfort object.
	3 Cooperates with caregiving experiences (e.g. dressing).
	4 Beginning to understand 'yes', 'no' and some boundaries.
Ages 16–26 months	5 Aware of others' feelings (e.g. looks concerned if hears crying or looks excited if hears a familiar happy voice).
	6 Growing sense of will and determination may result in feelings of anger and frustration (e.g. tantrums).
	7 Responds to a few appropriate boundaries, with encouragement and support.
	8 Shows they have learned that some things are theirs, some are shared and some belong to other people.
Ages 22–36 months	9 Seeks comfort from familiar adults when needed.
	10 Can express own feelings.
	11 Responds to feelings and wishes of others.
	12 Aware that some actions can hurt or harm others.
	13 Tries to help or comfort when others are distressed.
	14 Shows understanding and cooperates with some boundaries and routines.
	15 Can inhibit own actions/behaviours.
	16 Distracts self when upset (e.g. by engaging in new activity).
Ages 30–50 months	17 Aware of own feelings, knows actions and words can hurt others' feelings.
	18 Begins to accept needs of others, can take turns and share, sometimes with support.
	19 Tolerates delay when needs not immediately met and understands wishes may not always be met.
	20 Adapts behaviour to different events, social situations and changes in routine.

6 The parents' perspective. What was learnt in the evaluation about working with parents, and what matters to parents?

Sue Greenfield

In this chapter, we look at the following:

- ■ The challenges of involving parents in the research and encouraging them to take part.

- ■ How does power impact on the gathering of information? Power and its importance in understanding the parents' perspectives.

- ■ The reality of the parents' backgrounds and the influence this had on relationships with staff.

- ■ The importance of parents knowing about the setting and the practitioners knowing about the lives of the children when they are not at nursery.

- ■ The impact of the Work Discussion group on the parents' relationships with practitioners. Did Work Discussion make any difference?

Introduction

This chapter is all about the parents and carers of the children who attend the nursery. I reflect on the importance of their role, their relationships with the practitioners, the challenges they face in their daily lives and the way this is all connected to the Work Discussion group. We thought that we wanted to include the parents in this project and ask them about the Work Discussion, as their views could be set alongside those of the practitioners when considering ways of engaging parents in the setting and how information was exchanged.

The *Statutory Framework for the Early Years Foundation Stage* (Department for Education, 2021a) highlights the importance of 'partnership working between

DOI: 10.4324/b23247-8

practitioners and with parents and/or carers' and that 'children benefit from a strong partnership' yet provides little guidance as to how this can be achieved. The relationship between the practitioners and the parents appears to be crucial in promoting ways that nursery and home can work together, which in turn promotes children's learning. The relationship between the practitioners and the parents appears to be crucial in promoting ways that setting and home can work together. Crozier and Davies (2007) suggest where there is not a 'sharing of views and ideas', there may be a hidden understanding that 'parents are not valued' (ibid:311). The aim is to try to find out whether or not the Work Discussion group can play a part in fostering this relationship by enabling practitioners to understand ways they can relate to all of the parents and make them feel valued so their voices are heard. We wanted to find out if they shared views and ideas with each other.

The challenges of involving parents in the research

It was not merely as easy as 'go and ask the parents', and at first, parents were reluctant to take part in the research. We were very mindful from previous experience, of the obstacles facing parents. We were sensitive to the anxieties that an invitation to take part in research may provoke. Some were not confident to take part because their first language was not English, others because their time was taken up with a number of issues impacting on their lives and on their children. I say a bit more about this later on. I spent time in the nursery to try to get to know the parents, meeting them and answering their queries. The staff helped by organising the times of the interviews of parents who agreed to be involved. Though some parents signed up to take part, they did not turn up at the allotted time or, in some cases, at all. We tried to reassure them that our research would be confidential – we were not employed by the nursery or the government or local authority, and their identity would never be revealed – but they remained cautious and reluctant to become involved. We needed to take a different approach, so we offered to visit parents/carers at home rather than carry out the interviews in the setting. They assured us they would prefer to be interviewed in the setting. We then asked if they would prefer to be interviewed in small groups which was much more popular and gave us access to a larger number of parents. The parents spoke a wide range of languages, and the group scenario allowed those who were not too confident speaking in English to gain support and encouragement from others. In total, 19 different parents participated, eight in the first round and a further 11 by the second.

How does power impact on the gathering of information?

The hidden power in the relationships between the practitioners, the parents and the researchers is demonstrated by the way that parents used their power to decline to take part in the research at the beginning. The existence of power has an impact on what we wanted to find out and subsequently on the truths provided by the parents. The parents did not have to tell us everything they felt; they could choose their own version of the truth. We knew that it may influence all the people involved in contributing to our research, but the people involved do not always realise the impact it is having on the decisions that they make and the ways they react. These are some examples of situations where power may have an influence.

Health Services/Social Services – setting

Some of children attending the setting had been referred by Social Services or Health Services. They had not freely chosen to attend the setting but had been told by those in authority such as social workers or health visitors to bring their children to the setting. They had no choice about this. Inevitably, this influenced how parents/carers felt about the setting and those who work there. These parents may be wary of the setting and staff feeling they were under surveillance. They would be reluctant to criticise anything in case it had detrimental outcomes for either them or their children. These parents/carers may have become wary of 'authority' figures in their children's lives because of difficult relationships with these figures in the past.

Parent – Practitioner

Parents had the power to hold/withhold information about their circumstances and their children. They may not have wanted to share their knowledge, even though they are the experts on their children and all the details that they know can make a difference to the ways their children relate to a new setting. It is very helpful to staff to know a little about how the child is at home and what their background is. For example, a child who lives in a flat with no outside space may have little opportunity to run and jump, whereas a child who has access to outside space would have this opportunity. It has frequently been demonstrated that where home and setting work together, the outcomes for children are better (Knopf and Swick, 2007). However, parents only disclose what they want to disclose, and they can decide what is important for them and for their children. They may not want to divulge confidential information. They can choose whether to attend a session or not, but there is always the feeling that whatever they do, there may be consequences for their child. Parents may not be sure about trusting the practitioners and may feel judged.

The practitioners have the power of professional knowledge and the 'protection' of the institution and their colleagues. Their professional bodies decide on expectations and outcomes. They use English as the dominant language. The children have a wide variety of cultures and backgrounds. Are these practitioners aware of the effect this may have on, for example, language development where English is not the first language? They decide which children will move rooms and who will not; they assess the children to help them make these decisions.

Researcher – Parent

The parents can choose whether to take part in the research or not. They see the researcher as 'authority figure' who may divulge information to setting or to Social Services or Health Services. It is difficult to explain the researcher role, especially to those for whom English is not the first language or to convince them of confidentiality. The researcher decides on the questions, uses English for the interviews and decides on location which initially was a room in the setting. Interestingly, when given the choice to meet at the setting or at home, ALL the parents choose the setting.

Researcher – Practitioner

It is important to consider how the practitioners perceive the researchers and their presence in the setting. The research days were arranged with the Head of the setting, and the practitioners circulated the invitations about the interviews to the parents. The practitioners, who are in charge of organising the interviews, could choose who to invite. They probably know some parents well, and these may be the ones who are invited, but there are other parents who are much less well known or less involved. This poses a query about whether or not this will have an effect on the outcome of the research. There are always some parents who are not known as well or not seen very often in the setting (Swick, 2004), and these may easily be missed and left out. The practitioners also decide where the interviews should take place. This may not always be somewhere where people can be put at ease.

Which parents?

Our research aimed to obtain the views of a wide range of parents. It is well documented that those who become involved in settings are the parents who 'fit' (Knopf and Swick, 2007). Two parents interviewed were employed in the setting, and others were well known to staff, as they had had other children in the nursery or had attended one or more of the extra groups organised by the setting (e.g. English for Speakers of Other Languages). These parents were comfortable in the setting and related well to the staff. Other parents who agreed to take part did not arrive at the time agreed, even though they were telephoned by the receptionist to remind them. This clearly demonstrates the power of the parents to make the final decision about taking part in the research. These parents certainly come from a 'variety of sociocultural backgrounds' and are those whose children and identities should be honoured in a way that recognises and celebrates who they are (Souto-Manning and Swick, 2006).

Where?

The location for the interviews was problematic. All the rooms in the setting were much in demand, but an office with two hard chairs and a desk is not really an ideal place for an interview. The setting is one of being 'locked in' or 'locked out' for safety reasons which means that no one is able to 'wander in'. There is a large reception area, and the receptionists are very welcoming. Parents are anxious about me going to their homes, maybe because many are suffering deprivation and do not want anyone to visit at home. It could also be related to the lack of trust that some parents have in any 'figure of authority'.

What?

Parents often have issues that are worrying them, such as housing, missing families who live many miles away so they are not able to give support, low incomes and partners working very long hours. It is hardly surprising that they are pleased to have somewhere safe and warm, with welcoming staff, where they can leave their children for a while so they can try to solve some of the problems they face. Their situations gave no time for evaluation of the setting and staff.

What did we find out? The reality of parents' backgrounds

Getting to know the parents/carers of children attending a nursery is never easy. Parents have busy lives for many reasons. Nevertheless, our research gained an overview of just how difficult it was for these parents to provide the comfort and security they wanted for their children. These extracts from the parent interviews clearly demonstrate the challenges faced by the parents and things that all parents have to cope with on a daily basis. They live in an area that they find threatening at times, they have very little money and many live in one-bedroom accommodations with their partners and children.

This mother paints a dismal picture of the local area:

> but this area is so bad. You have prostitutes walking on the streets and drug gangs and still you can't find one bedroom flat under one thousand a month. It's horrible but I guess it's London. I'm on income support and I need three months guarantor for my flat it's such a lot of money. It's so bad for my kids' health. I have humidifier and I clean the flat constantly but all the flats are damp. I'm going to decorate again. . . . I have to decorate cos after the winter the mould has completely damaged it.

This mother explained how she felt she had to be out of the flat all day so there would not be any more complaints about the noise made by her son who has additional needs. In the summer, the family could go to the park, but in the winter, they just had to walk the streets, having no money to do anything else. The nursery has provided warmth and shelter for this little boy, who is making progress.

My son he didn't understand and my downstairs lady used to complain loads to the council and I keep telling her he doesn't understand. Now [he is attending here] it is much better and she is quiet. Hopefully they will find us a new flat because we have a one-bedroom flat with two children. It is very small. I can't take both of them outside because of my downstairs lady. I am telling everyone even you and hoping that someone can give me a letter so I can move.

Shared accommodation is another problem for several families:

We have to share with another family because when I was pregnant nobody wants children and we can't afford . . . He's very active, needs space. I have to do something with him. I can't keep in him in the house and if the weather is bad, we can't go to the park

The importance of parents knowing about the setting and the practitioners knowing about the lives of the children when they are not at nursery

Many of these parents had chosen the setting because of its good reputation in the area, and they pointed this out as the basis for their choice. Their relief at finding a warm, safe environment was very evident, as they commented on the contrast between their very stressful lives in very crowded and unsuitable accommodation and the supportiveness of the nursery. They welcomed the friendliness of the nursery and the way the staff greeted them and their children by name. Many had first visited the 'stay-and-play' sessions run by the nursery team as well as other group sessions, such as parenting classes and craft workshops, and some commented on how the nursery had reduced their isolation. The following quotes demonstrate the mothers' relief when they started attending the nursery, as they were no longer isolated. They could ask for advice and were made to feel at ease by the practitioner. One parent admitted that before she came to the nursery, she knew little about how to look after a baby. Her mother lived on the other side of Europe, and she had not yet made any friends. She had to look for answers on Google.

Even when you first walk in. Receptionist is friendly straight away and everyone is happy to help you. They always ask for your opinion as well. They ask what could we do to improve this and that. They make you feel really involved.

That's the thing when I was so isolated, before I came here. There was just the three of us. That's why he had so many issues and as soon as he came here, he could socialise and build up his confidence. For me it is much nicer.

This mother had just left an abusive relationship and praised the way the nursery supported her:

His key worker noticed and she always tried to talk to me and she understands cos she grew up with problems in her family and she could look from the perspective of the child and she could understand. She grew up in a family [who] was not involved and she had to make a decision to cut off the [her] father. She really supports me in every way.

These very positive comments could be built on by the practitioners, but it seems that parents often either did not feel confident to have more than superficial discussions with practitioners or have the time to do so. Practitioners, too, had little time to have meaningful discussions with parents, as they are busy working with the children. Both parents and practitioners gave each other the impression that they were 'busy', but this could have been a way of avoiding more meaningful interaction.

Communicating with the nursery

The parents were asked about their interaction with the practitioner at the nursery. It was obvious that this was not always easy, as this mother points out:

I came here eleven years ago and I couldn't speak English at all. If people can't speak English, how can they tell their children [what to do] or speak to other people

As many of the parents had a language other than English as their first language, communication was not always easy, and though practitioners could give parents some ideas of how their children were progressing, this was not always successful. Some parents made it clear that their understanding was not very good, while others who appeared to understand did not.

This mother spoke little English, yet she was very happy with her experience of the setting and her Key Person:

Yes, they look after her very well and J is very good she knows everything. My daughter had a rash and she ask for cream. They look after her very well. We trust her and our child is very precious. We trust them.

Only one parent of the 19 gave an indication that he did not have trust in the practitioner:

> but we've been misinformed. Like have they decided not to tell me what's happening there like someone pushes her – I'm not saying they do – and she gets a graze on her knee they might say 'oh she just fell over'. I'd rather know that somebody pushed her rather than she just fell over because. . . . I just would, you know what I mean.

This was in one of the initial interviews and certainly demonstrates a lack of trust and communication, but the views expressed are in stark contrast to other parents who stated that they were very happy with the friendly and caring practitioner as seen earlier.

Parents' awareness of the Key Person role

All the parents were aware of their Key Person (a named practitioner responsible for a small group of children and families), and many spoke very highly of them:

> He was very sensitive then and now he's very confident he plays with other children, he's just very happy. I've been very lucky with my key worker as well cos she has proper connections with the children and S just really loves her. I'm just worried about next year cos he will have another key worker now and I'm worried about the separation.
>
> Yes she (my key person) lets me know what is going on. What my daughter did. If there's anything going on I let her know. My daughter loves her. She is really kind.

However, the links between home and setting and vice-versa seemed to be very limited. When parents were asked if they knew what their children did at nursery each day, they knew what the children had eaten or whether or not they had slept but did not appear to know about friends or activities. There are two possible reasons for this: firstly, they may not have been told, but secondly, they may not have considered this to be important. When asked about their children's activities at home, many mentioned television or iPad and that they were pleased their children were away from these when at nursery. They certainly valued the space provided by the nursery, especially the outdoor area. Interestingly, all parents said that they rarely discussed their home activities with practitioner.

It seems that the relationships with practitioners were often on a superficial level; parents were happy with the physical space and the activities provided but had not really built up close and trusting relationships with the practitioners. They did not share their worries about their situations, even though these were so closely related to their children.

What was the impact of the Work Discussion group on the parents' relationships with practitioners

I have worked directly with parents as both a practitioner and researcher over nearly forty years. While carrying out this research, I found it hard to come to terms with the isolation and hardship experienced by parents whose families were many thousands of miles away. They had moved to the UK in search of 'a better life' and coped with their daily struggles without complaint. These parents were coping with many difficulties, and this is in common with many other families whom I was not able to interview.

The research interviews were intended to explore the relationship between the parents and the practitioners to see if a partnership was developing between them and whether or not the Work Discussion had helped. The primary finding in relation to this question is that we cannot be sure. We now wonder if partnership, particularly given the challenging circumstances these parents were often facing, could ever exist given how much both parents and practitioners would need to invest in such a relationship to be it a reality. The relationship between parents and practitioners is crucial, but the most important aspect seems to be trust. In spite of the fact that the parents interviewed had so many stresses in their lives, they knew the importance of having practitioners who cared about their children and who could be trusted to look after them with kindness and understanding without necessarily having detailed frequent exchanges of information between home and nursery. The parents seemed happy about the setting from the beginning, and they were pleased to have a warm and caring environment that was a contrast to their often uncomfortable and stressful home surroundings. The nursery was warm and inviting and safe.

There was evidence of a lack of shared information between home and setting and between setting and home. Parents were unsure about what happened at nursery and did not share much information about their home environments with practitioners. The Work Discussion group could be an ideal opportunity to enable practitioners to reflect on this. Of course, it could be that parents did not want to discuss their home situations with practitioners, but they had no hesitation in doing so with the researcher interviewing them.

Though there is no direct evidence that the Work Discussion groups improved relationships between practitioner and parents. It was much easier to persuade parents to be interviewed in the last rounds of interviews towards the end of the year-long period of field work. This could be because the practitioner approach changed as a result of the Work Discussion group which allowed time for them to reflect on the families they worked with. Parents were more pleased to take part. Equally, it may have been that growing familiarity with the researcher and her presence in the nursery encouraged parents to be more open. Growing familiarity and trust between parents and practitioners is crucial.

PART THREE
Nursery Leaders talk about their experience of Work Discussion

7 Research into Practice. Inviting Nursery Leaders to try out Work Discussion

What did they make of it?

Ruth Seglow and Peter Elfer

Giving serious attention to feelings as part of nursery work

Ruth is a Child Psychotherapist with long experience of working in and consulting to nurseries. Peter is a researcher who has spent many hours in nurseries, being allowed to observe and listening to nursery practitioners talk openly about their work. We both have experienced how strongly feelings feature as part and parcel of nursery life. Thank goodness for that! The idea of a nursery without feelings is horrifying! Nobody would want children with adults who were robots.

Nursery practitioners' accounts of nursery life are full of feelings – happy, affectionate feelings from children and the satisfaction and joy of seeing children grow. But there are other kinds of feelings, too, including ones of worry, upset, frustration, and sometimes anger. How does the practitioner deal with that? A child may be upset when left at nursery, and then the practitioner, trying to comfort that child in the absence of the parent, is roughly pushed away by the child. It can feel very rejecting to the practitioner to be rejected by the child. We would not expect that any practitioner would retaliate and push the child back, although they may well feel like doing it. A good practitioner will, of course, not retaliate. For many practitioners, receiving negative feelings, of all kinds, from children is a daily experience. However careful the practitioner is to remain professional and try and not let her own feelings show, we do not think it is a nursery practitioner's role to be a kind of 'punchbag'. We think that practitioners need an opportunity to air these feelings away from the children and be supported to think about them with colleagues. The feelings are then less likely to leak out in other ways. If feelings can really be thought about, they become transformed. That is important for the quality of pedagogy. And it is important for the wellbeing of each practitioner too. Thinking about work situations, including the feelings they evoke, is the role of the Work Discussion group.

DOI: 10.4324/b23247-10

Research into Practice project

Following the research evaluation of Work Discussion (see Chapters 3, 4, 5, and 6 in Part Two), we approached the Froebel Trust to ask if they would fund a 'Research into Practice' project. The Trust spends a lot of money on research and wants this research, where appropriate, to make a positive difference to practice in the early years. The Trust calls this kind of link 'translational research'. We were thrilled that the Trust, having already provided funding for the WD evaluation, agreed to provide further funding for the 'Work Discussion Research into Practice' project.

The organisation of the project

This 'Research into Practice' project started in January 2020. We invited eight Senior Nursery Leaders, each one from a different kind of early years setting – for example, private nurseries, local authority Nursery Schools, preschools, and nursery classes attached to primary schools – to participate. We chose these leaders as ones who, if they were convinced about the value of Work Discussion, would be ones likely to be influential in supporting it for newer or less experienced practitioners. We asked each of the eight to come to a Work Discussion group and experience what it was like and whether or not they thought it could help them in their work. They were invited to 12 sessions, held at the Tavistock and Portman NHS Trust building in Swiss Cottage in North London (Dilys Wilson has talked about the Tavistock Centre in describing the development of Work Discussion in Chapter 2). In addition to the 12 sessions, there was one at the beginning for the leaders, all from different nurseries, to begin to get to know each other and to get to know us as the Work Discussion facilitators. Each of the 13 sessions lasted for one hour and a quarter, starting from 6:00 P.M. and ending at 7:15 P.M.

The Tavistock observation method

As the reader, you might be asking what is so special about the Tavistock Centre; it is not even an early years' education institution! We chose the Tavistock partly because it is the place where Work Discussion has developed and evolved over the last 50 years. Work Discussion has now been used in many different professions not only early years', for example, for doctors, teachers in secondary schools, teams in hospitals, and workers in probation.

Another reason for choosing the Tavistock is that it is the home of the Tavistock observation method. This method of observation has very particular features, where the observer does not use any kind of recording device but is asked to remember as much detail as possible about the whole experience of the observation. This includes the detail of the baby or child they have chosen to observe, both WHAT they do during the observation and HOW they do it and also includes the feelings the observer may have while they were observing. It is important to remember here that when we say 'feelings', we mean the emotions observers find themselves feeling as they observe. We do not mean 'feelings' in the sense of 'I felt this was bad practice' or 'I felt the parent was to blame'. Those are more judgements than feelings. The aim is to try and understand what may be occurring rather than to judge it as good or bad.

You as the reader may be thinking you have always been taught NOT to put feelings in your observations! There are good reasons for this in terms of being as objective as possible. But including feelings, for example, HOW a child did something, for example, with feelings of excitement and enthusiasm or reluctance and resentment, as well as WHAT they did, can be the key that unlocks our understanding of what was going on in that child's mind during the observation period.

Our eight Nursery Leaders were asked to do an observation of this kind for 20 to 30 minutes. We asked them to write it up and to bring it to the Work Discussion sessions, taking turns, so that each leader could present their observation and we could talk and think about it together.

The Covid pandemic and moving to meet online

We had only met briefly as a group at the Tavistock when the Covid pandemic hit. The eight Nursery Leaders had different views as to whether to postpone the Work Discussion groups until it was safe to meet in person again or to continue online. They decided in the end to continue online, using Zoom. Readers will know from their own experiences that being online, in small boxes on a screen, is a completely different experience from being together in person, as a face-to-face group, in a room. As you will read in the next chapters, with the Nursery Leaders' accounts of their experiences of the Work Discussion group, you will see, too, that it was much harder even to undertake the observations than before the pandemic.

What can you talk about in Work Discussion?

As Dilys Wilson has made clear in Chapter 2, Work Discussion is not a 'therapy' group for practitioners! The purpose is to support practitioners in their work to ensure as good as possible experiences for the children and families. However, it is not so easy to draw a clear line between what is appropriate and what is not! Some practitioners say you must leave your personal feelings at the nursery door. It would, though, be a very strange practitioner who really tried to do this and *to* work without any personal feeling. Personal feelings are with us all the time, at work and away from work. Things that happen outside our work are also bound to sometimes affect how we are at work however hard we may try not to allow this to happen. So helped by the Work Discussion group facilitators, Work Discussion groups need to be vigilant to ensure that whatever is discussed – whether about the practitioners themselves, the families, or the children they are working with – is done to support the team's work with the children and families.

Asking the Nursery Leaders to write about their experience in the Work Discussion group

At the end of the 13 sessions, we asked the eight Nursery Leaders whether or not they would like to write an account of their experience of the Work Discussion group. We wanted them to write honestly about their assessment of the strengths and difficulties of Work Discussion and whether or not they felt it made an overall contribution to the quality of their work with children and families and colleagues. Five of the eight said they would like to write about their experience of Work Discussion. The five were Christina, Emily, Tricia, Lisa, and Sam. Their stories about their experience of Work Discussion are in the next five chapters, Chapters 8–12.

Experiencing a Work Discussion group

Christina

The influence of a charismatic lecturer

If you are reading this as an early years' practitioner, I wonder what you think are the influences in your life that have made you the practitioner you are. There are probably many, maybe your own growing up, maybe training, maybe a colleague or manager. For me, it was a lecturer called Mary. I always felt empowered by her teaching. Our other lecturers were usually limited to strictly meeting the subject criteria, and there was little space to digress into thinking about and sharing the influence on professional practice of personal experiences. Mary told us that once, she had had the privilege of meeting John Bowlby, the architect of attachment theory. The feeling with which she described his work made a deep impact on me. I will never forget the understanding she had gained from him of the vital importance of the bonds young children make with individual early years practitioners, as well as with family members. Overall, Mary introduced us to the importance of feelings in learning to become early childhood pedagogues and in early childhood pedagogy.

We have many experiences in our lives that contribute to the practitioners we become. But only a few provide that passionate feeling of what really matters in our work with young children. For me, it was about how much relationships matter and how important it is for us to think about children's feelings in these relationships. That is what Work Discussion is all about, noticing passionate feelings in children and also noticing all the varieties and subtle shades of feeling, as well as feelings that stand out.

Being observed, being observed observing

We were asked to bring an observation of a child to the Work Discussion group, and I felt excited and enthusiastic about this and was looking forward to sharing it with the group. However, with the onset of the Covid pandemic, my feelings of elation soon diminished, as my focus, in terms of the group, was now centred on how I was going to complete my observation. When I was put on furlough along with many of my colleagues, I was not only thinking of how this affected

DOI: 10.4324/b23247-11

my working life and that of my colleagues but also of the children and parents in our care, as well as how this would impact on my further involvement with the Work Discussion group. I was not able to observe in my own nursery (because my nursery was closed during the pandemic) and so decided to ask another nursery manager whether or not I could undertake my observation in her nursery via a Zoom link. I was not prepared for the time it took for me to secure a date and time for the observation. I found myself questioning why my colleagues in the nursery where I was to observe, knowing my commitment to my role, were not being more forthcoming in helping me to find a way to observe whilst isolating at home. Was it rather naive of me to think my problems were in any way, shape, or form a priority for them? After many days of waiting for a response, I knew that the request meant very little to them and did not warrant their immediate attention. They were currently dealing with a lot of uncertainty and anxiety to do with trying to maintain a service for working parents in the midst of Covid. The time frame for the Work Discussion group to do their observations was running out, and I found myself becoming more and more frustrated, exacerbated by the fact that I was at home and facing uncertainty myself about what lay ahead. The Work Discussion group was helpful and supportive here, enabling us to reflect deeply on the different nursery situations confronting us. I felt our work together enabled me to be more patient and understanding, helping me manage my increasingly difficult feelings.

After a few weeks, I finally received confirmation that I would be allowed to undertake my observation at the setting of my choice. I had made this particular choice of nursery because I was very keen to observe a child called Victoria, who had previously been at my setting. I chose to observe Victoria, who was 13 months old at the time of the observation (May 2020), because she was familiar to me and because I was missing her so much. Here was my opportunity to see her and catch up with how she was doing since I had last seen her two months earlier. Due to the Covid lockdown, she had moved from my nursery setting to one of the other nurseries in the organisation. Victoria started at our nursery when she was 7 months old. She attended three long sessions each week (9:00–5:00 – Wednesday to Friday). She was always content and happy to separate from her mother (who, as a key worker during Covid, was continuing to work).

EDITORS' REFLECTIONS BOX 1: WHAT DOES IT FEEL LIKE TO OBSERVE, AND WHAT INFLUENCES THE OBSERVATION?

In Christina's account earlier, she talks a lot about feelings and about how influential a lecturer called Mary was in Christina's own training and development as an early years' practitioner. She is also honest about her feelings of frustration as she struggled to get the nursery to set up the observation for her on Zoom. Part of the difficulty was that she wanted to observe a particular child called Victoria, who used to be in her own nursery but because of Covid, had transferred to a different nursery. We want to acknowledge her patience and her understanding about what a difficult time it was for the nursery staff too. Christina says that she wanted to observe Victoria because she was missing her and wanted to have the chance to see her and see how she was getting on. Inevitably, we always bring the feelings from any relationship we have had with a child to the observation of that child. So an important point here is what are the factors that influence the mindset we bring to an observation. Christina wants to observe Victoria because she understandably misses her. For example, does an early years' practitioner 'see' a child differently with whom they have had a positive relationship from how they 'see' a child with whom they have had a more challenging relationship?

The joy and sadness of observing Victoria

The observation day arrived, and as the nursery room came into view, there seemed to be quite a distance between Victoria and the screen. (Was I overthinking things when I began to question whether or not the arrangements for the observation were good enough, with the laptop far enough away from the children not to be a nuisance but close enough to see?)

At the beginning of the observation when I saw Victoria, I felt a wave of sadness because in front of me on a small laptop screen was a child with whom I had previously had very close interactions and knew very well:

Victoria is sitting on the floor next to a table, an adult is nearby. This particular adult is not her usual Key person but one of the staff members who has been looking after her over the last two months. Victoria reaches out and grabs hold of the table leg and uses it to pull herself up to a kneeling position. She then puts both hands onto the tabletop and attempts to pull herself into a standing position. At this point I found myself willing for her to stand, as I had not seen her do this before and it would be another milestone in her physical development. I wondered if she had already mastered this during her time at this new setting. Just as she reaches the full standing position, she loses her balance and drops down. Victoria makes a small crying sound as her bottom hits the floor. I move closer to the screen and say 'Well done Victoria' knowing she cannot hear or see me but eager for her to be consoled by my voice. In the past, the baby room at our setting was next to my office and I would always see and talk to her.

EDITORS' REFLECTIONS BOX 2: NOT TOO CLOSE, NOT TOO DISTANT – WHERE DOES THE OBSERVER POSITION THEMSELVES?

In this situation of observing remotely, Christina had the difficult job of observing from outside of the nursery using Zoom and a laptop. It is easy to imagine how frustrating this could be for Christina, as she wanted to see and hear the details of Victoria's play and interactions in the nursery, as well as get a sense of her feelings within each tiny interaction. Yet she often moved away from the field of view of the computer camera. What an almost impossible task for Christina! We admire her persistence in keeping the observation going and the actions of the staff working with Victoria in enabling this. However, even observing directly within a nursery brings challenges and difficult questions of judgement about where the observer should position herself. (We recognise that many observations are now done by practitioners as they work, and they will not be in only one position. We, however, are recommending a different kind of observation – see Chapter 7.) In any nursery room, the observer must decide the best position to place herself so that she is near enough to hear and feel but not so close as to be intrusive. Done in this way, the observer has much clearer and more detailed information with which to think about an individual child in a Work Discussion group.

Victoria now had unfamiliar adults interacting with her, and I knew that the bond she had formed with me, and her original Key Person, would soon become a distant memory. Throughout the observation, I acknowledged any challenges she overcame with gentle whispers and gestures towards a small screen which, regrettably, was not visible to her. My familiar voice could not be used to console any upset and frustrations she was experiencing due to my voice being muted and communication with the adults in the room not being possible. I found this virtual observation to be increasingly upsetting and difficult and wondered if I should give up and request the possibility of a face-to-face contact. Thankfully, perseverance and commitment got the better of me, and I continued to make the best of a challenging and very impersonal situation. I questioned why I was finding this particular observation challenging. I recognised that the emotion I was experiencing was borne out of me finally acknowledging that Victoria would no longer be a part of our setting, and I wanted them to provide the same 'Professional Love and care' (using a term drawn from the work of Jools Page[1]) she had experienced before. It was a sad realisation that due to this unexpected disruption (Covid) in all our lives, I would no longer play a part in Victoria's educational journey. I was elated to see Victoria was still the same inquisitive little girl I had known her to be. During the observation, she continued to be full of curiosity and explored her new learning environment with the same awe and wonder I had often witnessed in our setting. A moment during the observation led me to question my patience once again. At one point during the observation, Victoria disappeared from view when she moved towards the end of the room. I remember anxiously looking for my phone, locating it and dialling the setting's number. I was reliant on the phone being answered immediately and swift action being taken to allow the observation to continue. Thankfully, the wait had not been too long, and very soon, the manager was able to come and reposition the laptop. I fully understood that this was a visual observation and knew, out of professional courtesy, I would be mindful not to interrupt the children's learning.

EDITORS' REFLECTIONS BOX 3: THE IMPORTANCE OF ATTACH-MENT AND LOSS IN THE NURSERY

We think Christina has described her deep feelings for Victoria very well. She is desperate to see her and to feel the same connection with her that they had formed when she was in her nursery. It is easy to see how important she is to her and to imagine how much their relationship has meant to them both. The loss of it was felt to be unbearable. It is Covid that has disrupted their connection, as nurseries have closed. We think the kind of attachment that Christina is describing is very important for Victoria and for all children. We would describe it as 'attunement' with a child's state of mind.

You could say that allowing children to get attached to you at nursery and the painfulness of losing those attachments is at the heart of early years work. It is work that can be full of deep satisfaction and joy, but loss and sadness are also part of the work. How do practitioners cope with these natural human feelings of attachment and loss? We say more about this in the next box, Box 4, and in Chapter 1.

In this Box, we have said something about how Christina's attachment to Victoria has affected her as she does her observation of Victoria. Christina could not have been prepared for the intensity of feeling she experienced when observing Victoria. In essence, it was Christina's 'goodbye' to Victoria, now she is settled in another nursery, but without Victoria 'being there' to say goodbye to her in person and for Christina to see how she responds and to help her with her response.

Thinking about Victoria in the Work Discussion group

The day had finally arrived for me to present my observation to the group. I was surprised how anxious I felt about presenting it, whether or not it would be seen as a 'good-enough' observation of Victoria to enable the group to get to know her. Even though I was familiar with the Work Discussion group by now, this session would put me into the spotlight, and I was anxious to see whether or not my observation would spark an interest and further understanding in them about her.

The group could hear the emotion in my voice as I referred to Victoria's interest in a display of photos of family and other important attachment figures of each of the nursery children next to the mirror and emphasises the importance of the link between their home and nursery community:

> Victoria turns her attention to the photos displayed next to the mirror. She crawls toward it and begins to tap on the photographs. She moves very close to one of the photos and touches it with her mouth – could she be attempting to kiss the photo? I wondered at this moment whether Victoria was possibly looking for a photo of her mum or dad. I began to think about the lovely photos we had at our Nursery and how Victoria could often be seen looking at her mum and dad's photos. Had she spotted a photo that was familiar to her?

Could the previous text be interpreted as her desire to seek out a familiar face from her own family? I very much hoped that Victoria's family photos would soon be displayed in the room of her new nursery to help her feel secure in this new learning environment. The group talked about Victoria's verbal and non-verbal communication (remember, Victoria is only 13 months old) and how it differed from the other observations we had heard in the group where clear, identifiable language had been recorded. The language and gestures Victoria used were often open to interpretation, and educated guesses were being made by me and others in the Work Discussion group as to what she wanted and how she was feeling. My understanding and emotional reactions were based on what I already knew and had seen Victoria demonstrate several times (but, of course, other members of the group, coming from different nurseries, did not have this prior knowledge of, and relationship with, Victoria).

We had now reached a point in our Zoom sessions where the group facilitators made space at the beginning of the Work Discussion sessions to invite us to reflect on how we were feeling and if and how managing our work with the children was being impacted by the pandemic. As each session went by, we, the Work Discussion participants, experienced more and more the effects of the pandemic and the stress and anxiety it produced about how to work as safely as possible with the children.

We fell deeper and deeper into our discussions, with the group confiding in each other about their own personal experiences and feelings. Emotions were rife, and I felt that the Work Discussion facilitators were put in the position of supporting the group emotionally but, at the same time, ensuring that there was adequate time allocated for our observations.

It was a very difficult time and, on reflection, raised the question about how much personal feelings of the practitioners in relation to their work should be talked about in Work Discussion. I strongly believe that they should be because our present circumstances had completely changed our original objective. I felt the mindset we were all bringing to the sessions was slowly being impacted by our 'new normal' situation of working within the constraints and risks of the pandemic.

EDITORS' REFLECTION BOX 4: THE PERSONAL FEELINGS OF PRACTITIONERS IN RELATION TO THEIR WORK

We want to question Christina's view that our original objective was 'completely changed' by the pandemic. Our view of Work Discussion is that it very much concerns the impact of anything on the life of the nursery because that will have an impact on the feelings of the practitioners, and this inevitably will have an impact on the children in their care. Some readers may say that there would not be an 'inevitable' impact on the children be-cause a good practitioner should leave their personal feelings at the nursery door. How-ever, practitioners are, after all, human as well as professional. We think that, however hard they try and leave their feelings outside the nursery, feelings do tend to leak out, and children are very sensitive to picking up on how adults are feeling. Work Discussion aims to help practitioners contain their natural feelings, whether for example of love and at-tachment, or more difficult feelings arising from within or outside the early years setting.

In the situation that we were in, the preoccupation of the group was with the stress and anxiety in their work caused by Covid, but it could easily have been anything else. Inevitably, our world had changed forever from pre-Covid days.

Conclusion: benefits and drawbacks from participating in a Work Discussion group

In conclusion, I believe that, for me, my decision to be part of the Work Discussion group allowed me to fully embrace and participate in a new type of reflective practice and critical thinking I had not experienced before. Most importantly, it provided an opportunity for me to look closely at my role as an early years' educator and how I will continue to support my colleagues and the children in my care. The sessions allowed us to evidence our individual thought processes in response to what was being shared, discussed, and evaluated. Through our weekly discussions, I gradually experienced an emotional connection with the other participants and knew this would benefit my individual learning in the weeks ahead. For our project to be successful, I believe it was imperative that the facilitators provided an environment where we could come together as equals and where our individual experiences would be respected and valued.

However, in-depth thinking always carries the risk of touching on uncomfortable feelings, and people joining a Work Discussion group need to be prepared for this. For nursery practitioners, when they join a Work Discussion group, they may wish to present a situation in their nursery that is difficult or not going well, for example, with a child or family. Trying to understand this better in the group inevitably involves looking at the feelings of everyone who is involved – parents, child, and nursery practitioners, including oneself. They may find themselves feeling and showing a vulnerability about something that had happened in the nursery.

The facilitators are there to help the Work Discussion participants manage and be supported at these times. The understanding and empathy shown by the group helped to guide the decisions participants made and allowed them to feel less uncomfortable in their vulnerability.

EDITORS' REFLECTION BOX 5: VULNERABILITY

Our view about this vulnerability is that it comes when adults are in touch with any child's painful feelings and that bearing the vulnerability is about bearing the child's feelings. We think this can only be helpful to the child.

In terms of any drawbacks, I feel that full participation is beneficial to a Work Discussion group. When signing up for the group, you make a commitment to attend every session.

As time went on, the group met with remarkable consistency given the difficulty of meeting at all during the Covid pandemic when everyone was so worried about personal safety, the wellbeing of others, and their drastically changed work circumstances. We were also in the much less comfortable situation of 'meeting' in the small squares of our computers on Zoom, as opposed to getting to know one another in a circle in a room, as we had begun to do in our first few sessions before the pandemic struck.

Note

1 Page, J. (2018) Characterising the principles of Professional Love in early childhood care and education. *International Journal of Early Years Education*, 26(2), 125–141. https://doi.org/10.1080/09669760.2018.1459508

Experiencing a Work Discussion group

Emily

The complexity of working with young children

I initially started working with young children in early years and primary schools as an early years assistant and teaching assistant. After qualifying as a primary school teacher, specialising in early years, I worked as an early years teacher in a Sure Start Children's Centre. My current role includes teaching on further education and degree early childhood programmes in a college alongside spending time in our on-site nursery for children aged 3 months to 5 years.

As I have spent more time with young children, my wonder at the capacity for infants, toddlers and young children to explore their world, communicate, make meaning and form loving relationships has increased. I see being part of their lives in many ways a privilege. These statements are true and yet, are only telling part of the story. Perhaps the part of the story that most of us only feel comfortable sharing – influenced by some unwritten rule of always being positive that governs what we share about our work with children.

So even though we recognise children as not being one homogenous group and explicitly value their unique needs, recognise their personal experiences and promote their individual voices, we often summarise our experiences working with children as though our experiences with all children are distinctly similar, that our experiences are almost always fulfilling and positive. This does not, however, genuinely acknowledge the complexity of working with children; the difficult relationships with children and families; the disconnect we feel with some children and their families; and the feelings of unhappiness, unsatisfaction and, dare I say it, dislike. Pretending we, and the children and families, do not have these feelings does not mean they do not exist. However, we tend to shy away from these difficult emotions, acutely aware of how we will be perceived if we shared them with others.

DOI: 10.4324/b23247-12

EDITORS' REFLECTIONS BOX 1: 'BEING POSITIVE . . . AND DARING TO DISLIKE'

We think Emily makes an extremely important point in her reference to 'dislike'. Human relationships will INEVITABLY always involve some feelings of dislike towards some people, children or other adults. Some practitioners might find themselves feeling critical of this reality. They might argue that there should be no place in early childhood practice for a practitioner who may at times have feelings of dislike for a child's behaviour and even the child themselves. We would WANT TO say that they are PROBABLY not being honest with themselves. We have never known a practitioner who did not do everything in their power to ensure that such feelings did not show. However, in life generally, as well as in our professional work, we cannot expect to like everyone all the time. It may seem like a dangerous thing to admit to, but it is true. That is why we think Emily is rather brave to acknowledge it.

As a new teacher, I worked in a Sure Start Children's Centre. Some of the children and families I worked with were experiencing extremely difficult and challenging circumstances. Looking back, I believe I was unprepared by my training for the emotive nature of the role, albeit, at the time, I was not consciously aware of this. Observing children, a curiosity about children's emotional worlds was ignited, and this was further reinforced, later, when studying for an MA in Early Childhood. I started to consciously wonder whether or not my training as a teacher guided me to consider cognitive aspects of a child's behaviour above and separate to the affective. The MA provided me with the language to articulate my own feelings and emotions and to begin to make sense of the behaviours I witnessed in others. This new ability to articulate enabled my capacity to think about, and process, the complexities inherent within all relationships, including those in the nursery with young children. Although, of course, this is important when supporting children and families in 'extremely difficult and challenging circumstances' as implied previously, I believe it is equally as important for the more 'ordinary' aspects of our day-to-day practice, for instance, the repeated exposure to the, at times, intense distress of young children's daily transition into the nursery world.

Observing feelings

Contemplating the emotive nature of the work of the practitioner, I began to question how we respond to children's distress, especially if we tend to shy away from difficult emotions ourselves. To tune into children's emotional worlds, we need to allow ourselves to be open to feeling emotions, both negative and positive. I believe that to do this effectively, we need space to have thoughtful discussions to explore our own, and children's, responses. Becoming aware of this, I was excited to participate in the Work Discussion project to learn more about the child's world, including their emotional world, and my own position as an adult in a nursery entering into children's worlds.

Who am I?

During the first Work Discussion session, the question '*Who am I?*' was raised. Reflecting on the Work Discussion project, I kept returning to this question. For me, it encapsulates the emotions and experiences I felt throughout the project. From our first meeting as strangers introducing ourselves (Who were we all?) to the sharing of our observations, where, for me, the following questions kept arising: Who am I as an observer? Who am I as a practitioner? How does who I am influence me as a practitioner? And finally, to the last meeting reflecting on how our worlds, the children's worlds, the parent's worlds, had unequivocally changed, as the world faced Covid, who am I now? And beyond Covid, who am I now as an evolving person and practitioner?

The question '*Who am I?*' was raised in the first Work Discussion session by the group member who was sharing her observation. It provoked discussion about how we should position ourselves during the observations. Unlike traditional observations, the observation method required us to watch the child in the nursery without taking any notes. Intuitively, I wanted to write *simply* watch here as, in basic terms, that is what it is: you are *simply* watching the child, but the observation experience itself paradoxically feels anything but simple. The experience of observing and sharing in the Work Discussion group often being an emotive experience for myself and the other members, notably, there were times when members became upset discussing a situation. However, equally, there were times of shared laughter (recalling times of joy with children) and shared anger (for example, about the lack of clear guidance for the early years sector in managing Covid).

Even the process of conducting the observations, *simply* watching was complicated by my feeling a heightened awareness of wanting to be seen to be 'doing it'. The strangeness of observing and not taking notes made me feel conscious of being judged by the other practitioners. Interestingly, I had had prior experience of undertaking this type of observation. However, previously, I was observing as a 'researcher'. The notion of sitting back and watching felt more conspicuous when working with the children. This made me wonder why, generally, the appearance of busyness in practice seems to be valued and, personally, why I feel the need to be busy, to be doing something. Part of me believes we strive to be seen as busy, as we equate 'busy' with being professional, influenced by the neoliberal notion of 'hard work pays'; and therefore, the 'busier' we are, the more 'value' we have. However, reflecting on my own experiences of the observation method, I wonder how we might use 'busyness' to protect ourselves from being too open to the feelings and emotions of others. The idea that we should not distract children from their emotions and feelings is becoming well established; but is it not also possible that we may distract ourselves from being overwhelmed by others' emotions that we distract ourselves through busyness? Thus, the pen and paper in a typical observation acts as not only a physical barrier but an emotional one too. And so I would argue that to embrace this new way of observing, you need to be willing to accept your own vulnerability to being open to the children and, consequently, allowing yourself the time to truly notice them.

EDITORS' REFLECTIONS BOX 2: ON 'WHO AM I?'

Emily points so helpfully to the different roles she experiences as a practitioner – always being the private person she is but also being a professional, sometimes leading, sometimes following, sometimes more active, sometimes more standing back and observing. Others in the Work Discussion group raised this, too, asking the question 'Who am I?' Of course, every practitioner plays all these roles with shifts more towards one role and then more towards another.

Observing based on the Tavistock observation method (see Chapter 7), where the observer does not have any notepad or other recording device but is trying to get right into the shoes of the observed child, seeing through the child's eyes, being receptive to what the child may be feeling, is not the easiest role to take. Emily asks about why 'the appearance of busyness' is so valued. It is a great question when being still and really trying to see things from a child's perspective is so valuable for the child. Feeling really seen and really understood is important for children. It is something many of us want for ourselves, although this can be a complicated business. Hopefully, we would want it, at least for the children in our care.

If we are to help children feel 'seen and understood', do we also need to have a professional space away from the children where we, too, can feel 'seen and understood' in our work?

By truly notice, I mean to pay attention to the small details, details that would not usually be recorded in an observation. I found now that not writing notes provided freedom to become more immersed in the child's world. Instead of time spent trying to formulate a sentence to describe what I had seen, I was in the moment with the child, not missing small behaviours due to looking down at a piece of paper. I observed Sophia, aged about 4 years. Although I knew Sophia spent most of her time in the nursery on her own, the observations enabled me to develop more awareness of Sophia's lived experiences at nursery, seeing behaviours I had not consciously noticed before. For example, the small moments where Sophia would glance at other children and the way he seemed to imitate the emotions displayed by other children even when not in close proximity to them:

She slightly lifts the train and then continues pushing it along the track until it reaches the end, before, again, moving in the opposite direction. When she reaches the end, she looks round the room for a moment. There is a group of children playing with the sand about half-way across the room. She straightens up as she watches them, her eyes seem very focused, she pokes out her tongue, lifting it as though she is trying to touch her nose with it. She looks like she is in deep thought. Sophia starts to collect pieces of train track and starts to extend the track; she intermittently looks up and watches the other children before returning to the task of building her track. She stops again to watch the children and one of them shouts excitedly. Sophia's body seems to tense in anticipation of the excitement. She smiles widely, teeth together in that excited/tense way. However, she does not move towards the children or attempt to interact. She does not look lonely or sad in any way, although, I felt a sense of sadness as I wondered if she wanted to join in with the other children – I was worried she was alone when she may have wanted to be part of their excitement.

Being in the moment with Sophia during this observation seemed to make me more open to her own emotional world. Although Sophia did not look upset about not being with the other children, I did sense a sadness; I felt it. However, this did result in a conflict for me. It raised two questions: (1) Was I feeling Sophia's longing to be with the other children in some way? Or (2) was I imposing my own feelings about how I would feel in a similar situation onto Sophia?

Making sense of what we see and feel

The more I reflected on these questions, the more I started to wonder about how we make sense of any behaviour we observe in children. I believe the meaning we make is always an interpretation. Therefore, I started to increasingly accept the complexity of being part of a child's world, especially their emotional worlds. Emotions are such that we will rarely, if ever, be able to ascertain someone else's subjective emotional experiences. They are often complicated further, as external reactions and behaviours can hide our true feelings. Yet we all make sense of our own lived experiences through our emotions. The conscious decision to identify and reflect on my own evoked emotions ultimately resulted in me becoming even more curious about Sophia, about her lived experiences within the nursery and about her emotional world. Thus, Sophia was increasingly held in my mind. So even though I cannot confirm whether or not it was Sophia's sadness that I felt, my feeling of sadness acted as a catalyst to learn more about Sophia's world, including her emotional experiences. I think it needs to also be acknowledged here that it is expected that you will not be certain about the origin of evoked emotions, especially at first. However, over time through repeated exposure as you continue with the observations, your attunement to the child's emotional world will be heightened. Beyond this, I think it is important to recognise how feeling held in mind itself is of immense value to the child. We do not need to always provide an answer; we do not need to always provide a solution to some problem. Feeling as though we are important to someone, that we are thought about and that someone really sees us and knows us helps us to feel valued and cared for. Ultimately, this is what children need – someone who knows them in the nursery world. For me, the observations resulted in my knowing Sophia. By this, I mean I started to have a deeper, more intimate knowledge of who she was. I noticed her more, and I would hold questions in my mind about her. Consequently, I believe this is of great benefit in practice to facilitate the making of meaningful relationships.

EDITORS' REFLECTIONS BOX 3: 'STARTING TO HAVE A DEEPER MORE INTIMATE KNOWLEDGE OF SOPHIA'

We would like to emphasise for the reader's attention what Emily has said about 'someone really knowing us'. There is such a difference between 'knowing about' someone (for example, what they physically look like, where they live, where they work, etc.) and 'really knowing someone' – the difference between reading about them and knowing them in person. The different kinds of observations required as documentary evidence to accompany a child's development in nursery are important and are a basis for feedback to parents. But they do not enable the same kind of 'knowing' that Emily is talking about here.

Emily does not mention this, but 'knowing' in the sense that she means may involve some quite tough, painful experiences for the practitioner. Children in nursery experience some very painful feelings as well as lots of joyous, wondrous ones. They need us to know about all their feelings, not only the ones that make us feel impressed, or inspired, happy or joyful. They need us to know, too, about their anger, sadness, worry and sorrow. These are not easy feelings to see and feel in another person, let alone in a young child.

We think it is not reasonable to expect early years practitioners to be alongside those feelings, with the depth of understanding that Emily describes, unless the practitioners also have a space away from the children to share some of the painfulness they have had to experience when seeing it in the children.

The observer becoming the observed!

Thinking about the observations with colleagues in the Work Discussion group. As someone who is naturally shy, I found the juxtaposition of the observer becoming the observed unnerving. My nervousness about reading out my observation interconnected with a sense of vulnerability that I would be exposing part of myself, both personally and professionally. A vulnerability, perhaps, heightened by prior commonplace professional experiences of scrutiny. I think it is not unfamiliar to anyone who has worked with children and, in education more widely, to have experienced systems of accountability that can feel unnecessarily intrusive and negative. Often our personal and professional selves are intertwined, and thus, exposing parts of our professional selves also has the potential to negatively impact our personal sense of self. Caring for others is often deeply personal even when in a professional role; the relationships built are often authentic and meaningful for practitioners as well as for the children. Therefore, we want to provide the best for the children we look after which is why I believe there is anxiety about sharing our practice: How will I feel if others judge my practice negatively when I care deeply about these children?

Although I initially felt anxious, the Work Discussion group became a space to not only talk about practice but to also acknowledge the messy – the uncertainty, the complexity, the difficult feelings. I think this is really important, as we often talk about practice on a day-to-day basis. We explain and justify our pedagogy within systems of accountability, but within these types of conversations, I have personally never experienced any acknowledgement of the complex nature of the role and the doubt that can sometimes exist. Accountability systems like simplicity; the certainty of one correct way feels safe and creates the illusion of control, but life is not dualistic (right or wrong) in nature and neither are our experiences. The Work Discussion group, in contrast, welcomes the element of uncertainty. As I discussed earlier, I was uncertain whether my feelings of sadness were from Sophia or from me; I did not leave the seminar group with an answer. In fact, I allowed the question to wallow in my thoughts. I no longer needed to ignore my own feelings but could accept them, listen to them and learn from them. What might my feeling be telling me about Sophia? What might my feeling be telling me about me?

Although the Work Discussion group does acknowledge and accept emotions, it is not a space where practitioners are self-indulgently talking about themselves for an hour. The process facilitates making meaning about the observed behaviours through thoughtful, detailed discussion. You are opening yourself up to other potentialities, alternative meanings than the ones you might have made. For me, the comments and questions posed by the other members of the group offered new insights that I had not personally considered, and the group provided a safe space for me to explore new perspectives. For example, when observing Sophia, I wrote:

> I feel more anxious than usual watching the interaction unfold and I wonder if it is because I am not only concerned about how the situation might escalate but about my own role within this situation – when do I step out of my observer role? I reason that usually when I pre-empt escalation, I would not allow so much time to sit back and observe how the children manage the situation alone. Perhaps, the uncertainty around my position as an observer and the uncertainty of what could happen adds to my own anxiety?

Discussing in the group my feelings that arise when faced with a potential conflict situation, notably anxiety centred on the uncertainty of the situation, I was able to reflect on my own vulnerabilities around conflict and how these influence my practice. Without thinking, I wrote about 'pre-empt[ing] escalation', not aware that others might wonder why I would pre-ompt it and that they did not routinely do this. It is important to note that the group are not interrogating you but genuinely asking questions to find out more about the situation so they can situate the observation within a wider context. This enables you to see the observation in a new light and to become aware of aspects that you thought were so obvious, they did not need to be written. This itself was something I found thought-provoking. It prompted new ways of thinking about the regularity of practice that is often so taken for granted, you do not even think it is worthy of being written down. And yet others were intrigued by it or needed to know more about it to make sense of a situation. For me, these new perspectives provided an opportunity for me to think about who I am and to be more conscious of the relationship between my own lived experiences and how these experiences influence my day-to-day practice, including my daily interactions and interpretations of events within the nursery world.

I feel fortunate that I was able to share my observation in our face-to-face Work Discussion prior to having to move online due to the Covid pandemic. Attending the group in person made me feel more at ease during our discussions. I believe the natural greetings as we arrived and the corresponding small talk prior to the discussion created a more comfortable environment to share my ideas with the group. Further, I found being confronted with ten faces watching me on a screen more exposing. This experience reinforced to me how in natural discussion, even when in a circle with the same ten people, you are not talking directly to everyone's faces; you tend to look at one or two faces at a time. That said, I did find the online discussions particularly useful during the first national lockdown for Covid. The Work Discussion enabled me to continue to be my 'professional' self, even when I could not be present at work. Further, there was a shared sense of vulnerability about the Covid situation and an opportunity to be seen and heard. During the lockdown, I was reading a book on vulnerability that identified a link between vulnerability and scarcity, stating that 'scarcity thrives in a culture where everyone is hyperaware of lack. Everything from safety to love to money and resources feels restricted or lacking' (Brown, 2012, p. 26). It made me consider the culture in Early Years of accountability, lack of funding, lack of protection and lack of value. The Work Discussion group often spoke of 'just getting on with it' as has always happened within the early years sector, a situation intensified by Covid. Feelings of anger were expressed at the lack of protection, care and value shown to nurseries during this time. Yet the group did let us be seen and heard beyond our own workplace environments, providing a feeling of 'worthiness' to counter the narrative of 'lack'.

Work Discussion as a way to develop a deeper understanding

Reflecting on my experiences of the Work Discussion project as a whole, I have found it to be valuable. The uniqueness of the Work Discussion observation resulted in me having a more intimate knowledge of Sophia; our relationship became richer. I spoke earlier about how I started to hold Sophia in my mind; in a similar way, I felt the Work Discussion group held the person sharing their observation in mind. Perhaps this is why when sharing your own observation, you are able to talk about the complexity, the uncertainty and the difficult emotions, as the group helped to contain some of the anxieties and vulnerabilities. Being given the space to acknowledge emotions helps to make sense of the experiences that we might usually push away as unacceptable. Looking back on my own practice, I know there have been times when I have felt exhausted by the intense emotions of others and so I started to become compassion fatigued; I could no longer contain others' emotions, as I was already too vulnerable from repeated exposure to these raw experiences of distress. For instance, when children start the setting, you are part of the child's, at times, overwhelming pain of being left by their parent. When many children are starting the setting at once, this can be physically and emotionally draining not only for the children and families but also for the practitioners. No wonder when we are in the day-to-day world of the nursery, many practitioners turn to distraction, both for themselves and the children. It is correct to advocate for the children and to recognise the importance of not distracting children from their emotions, but we have to practically, not only theoretically, recognise the dialogic nature of relationships. This means to support children emotionally, we need to support practitioners emotionally. I cannot contain the emotions of others if I cannot contain my own emotions. This is where I believe the value in Work Discussion lies. The Work Discussion group provides containment so that the practitioner can honestly identify and explore evoked emotions. I think most people can identify one or two people in their lives whom they turn to when they need to talk about something that is causing anxiety and/or difficult feelings. Often, we feel better once speaking through the situation. The Work Discussion group has the capacity to be that professional listening friend. It helps to hold the anxieties and vulnerabilities. That is not to say, however, that there is no critical discussion, that we all only respond with positiveness and niceties.

EDITORS' REFLECTIONS BOX 4: ON FEELING 'CONTAINED'

'Containment' is not a word used very much in early years writing. You may even find it a rather off-putting word, as it is often used in the media to mean a physical process or place, where people are held. It is a word though used in other professions, especially in child psychotherapy, where it is a fundamental idea. Like its everyday usage, it does have something to do with 'holding' but much more in a psychological sense than a physical one. We think Debbie Brace explains it beautifully:

> Receiving a child's distress means allowing the pain to be expressed, thought about and digested before the child is able to take back something more emotionally manageable. In a busy, early-years setting this can be a noisy, messy and draining process. Bion[1] calls this process containment (1962). Over time containment enables the child to internalise the experience of being cared for and feeling understood, and over time he or she is able to go on to notice, express and manage his or her own feelings in identification with the thoughtful, containing adult. This, according to Bion is one key to a mentally healthy life.
>
> (Brace, 2021, p. 4)

As Emily points out, Work Discussion is a professional space where practitioners can be part of providing that 'holding', or containment, for each other. Work Discussion is not a 'therapy' group! But it is a thoughtful professional safe space where both the painful as well as joyful feelings of early years work can be talked about and thought about, without anyone jumping to advise or to know better, but where practitioners can feel understood in their individual responses to the complex work that they are asked to do.

Questions are still asked to enable the group to discover more, to understand more about the situation/the behaviours/the evoked feelings and to make sense of what is being shared. Sometimes these questions and comments can evoke new difficult emotions with the group space affording an openness to explore these further. Thus, I believe there is a place for Work Discussion in early years settings, as it not only recognises the emotional labour of practitioners but validates the experiences by accepting the complexity of relationships within the nursery world. This is what a Work Discussion group should do. It should enable practitioners to make sense of their everyday experiences within a space capable of containing the anxieties and vulnerabilities that arise when exploring the difficult aspects of practice.

Note

1 Wilfred Bion (1897–1979) was a psychoanalyst who contributed hugely to our understanding of the processes of thinking and avoidance of thinking in groups.

Experiencing a Work Discussion group

Lisa

Observation as an emotional, transformational experience

I currently work as Deputy Head of a Federation of Maintained Nursery Schools in an inner city. I am also a visiting scholar at a university. I have spent my whole teaching career in the early years, having also worked as Early Years Consultant and Early Years Ofsted Inspector.

When asked to take part in the Work Discussion project, I was extremely keen. I had experienced using the adapted Tavistock observation method (this is explained in Chapter 7) as part of an MA module about observing the development of wellbeing in children under 30 months. The whole process of observing children closely and sharing the observation in the MA seminar group left a lasting impact on me. I described it at the time as 'intensely moving'. It was an emotional, insightful and transformational experience. It inspired me to lead significant improvements in staff reflection meetings at the Nursery Schools, engaging staff in more meaningful observations of children.

The 'more meaningful' observations, which had such a powerful effect on me, came about because observers were encouraged to notice the emotional state of the child they were observing and to record not only this but also the impact it had on them as an observer.

I also felt strongly that there was a huge gap in opportunities for supervision for leaders. Leaders are often committed to ensuring that the staff they work with have time to talk and reflect on the challenges of working with children, but they rarely have opportunities to address their own emotions, dilemmas and stresses.

I, therefore, jumped at the chance to further my knowledge about a model of professional reflection in which the emotions of the child, and the impact of these on the observer, were so central. The 'Work Discussion' meetings, with a group of eight professionals all working as leaders in the early years, started at the Tavistock Centre in London.

DOI: 10.4324/b23247-13

The value of 'great detail' in observation narratives

In our first session together, we listened to an observation about a 2-year-old, David, undertaken by Sam, another member of the Work Discussion group. As Sam read the observation to the Work Discussion group, it was clear that David was upset after saying goodbye to his mother. Reading the great detail of Sam's write up of her observation allowed the Work Discussion group to feel the sadness of the child. For example, the detached way in which David poked the playdough, looking up without expression when the Key Person spoke to him or to another child. The Key Person stayed with David, soothing him, and they walked together, hand in hand, towards some playdough:

> He starts to play, very tentatively, with the backs of his fingers at first . . . softly tapping the dough . . . David presses more firmly into the dough with his fingers, but his gaze remains down. The play continues but I note that David's level of physical involvement increases – he pokes the dough and the Key Person copies. He squashes the dough and again the Key Person mirrors. David's gaze remains mostly on the dough, but he occasionally glances up at the Key Person albeit with a fixed expression.

Despite the valiant attempts of David's Key Person, I was reminded just how emotionally challenging it is for the child to be at nursery. As we discuss the observation, the observer herself gets upset. I am touched by this level of emotion which powerfully highlighted the immense responsibility and pressures of working in the early years.

EDITORS' REFLECTIONS BOX 1: HOW MUCH THE 'GREAT DETAIL' MATTERS

In the paragraph earlier, Lisa talks about the 'great detail' of Sam's observation of David. What sort of 'detail' does Lisa mean here? She could be describing David's clothes in a highly detailed way, but this would not give us access to David's feelings. We want those listening to the observation to gain access to how the child observed may be feeling. We want access to the non-visible internal emotions of the child. In the context of Work Discussion, we are interested in descriptions that communicate how the child is *feeling*. The *way* in which the child behaves gives us valuable information about the *way* a child may be feeling.

This is what Lisa points to, in writing about Sam's observation of David.

Lisa draws attention to the particular details of language Sam uses, which evoke a picture of how sad David feels.

Being able to experience something of children's experience

Taking time to really feel the experiences of a child, as well as the emotional pressures on staff, helps us to reflect upon how we can support both children and staff in the best way possible.

When it was my turn to observe, I chose James, aged around 4, who was part of a close-knit threesome of children. In staff evaluation meetings, staff have commented that the children had been observed being 'unkind' to some of the more vulnerable children. James's mum told me recently that he had come home with quite a few small injuries. She said she knows that children can be unkind, but she asked us to keep an eye on it. This threesome was a group that many others wanted to play with, their physical skills and confidence making them appear popular and superior. I decided it would be useful to get a closer look at what was happening. The following is an extract from the observation of them in the home corner.

> There are two small sofas opposite each other. James sits on one, Mary on the other. James keeps moving his position and Mary copies. James sits on the arm of the chair, Mary copies. James bounces back down on the seat, Mary copies. It is like a mirror or a dance. James and Mary begin play fighting with the toy frogs they are holding. They are bashing each other's frogs.
>
> As I watch, it reminds of the animal kingdom, animals fighting for supremacy, I wonder if the children are also trying to work out the hierarchy in this threesome. To avoid being bashed, Mary holds her frog up high, she is taller than James who cannot reach so says, 'I want that frog'. Mary says 'no'. Meanwhile, Rik has been busy in the background pretend cooking – pouring pasta into saucepans. He comes over with a remote control and tells James and Mary 'I'm putting blaze on for you, watch it!' Mary takes the remote control from Rik who looks both saddened and resigned to this situation, He kneels down near Mary looking closely at her face as if trying to work out which tactic might work to get the control back. James also vies for the controller, telling Mary 'No, you don't press that, that pauses it'.
>
> I feel myself frowning, not liking the abuse of power. I notice Rik watching me. I am surprised by the intentness with which he is looking at me, his head to one side. He is watching me watching James. I can see that he is considering what I am thinking. As we catch each other's eyes, he smiles. The observer is being observed, I thought.

After carrying out the observation, I was aware what a luxury it was to gain such a window into the play and lives of these three children. As practitioners, we are rarely able to shut ourselves off to what is happening around us and focus on individual children for a sustained amount of time. We are constantly responding, interacting, multitasking. Putting oneself in observer role, in a closely attentive and receptive position, brings such great depth to our understanding of children. In times of such pace, pressure and stresses, it is a tool that allows us to refocus on what is important – children's lives and the detail of their feelings, relationships, joys and challenges. It helps us to create a place where we can see and feel child-hood, a place where childhood exists.

The discussion that followed in the Work Discussion group also helped me to reflect upon the different needs and interests of the three children – their interest and desire for competition, the active nature of their play and the different ways in which they learn. I was able to read through my observation with staff at my setting and relay the discussion that happened in the Work Discussion group. It helped us all to see the children with new eyes. We were able to be more sensitive to the ways in which we interacted with them to support their love of competition and har-ness the influence they had on other children in a positive way. For example, we appointed them 'the rescue squad', helping other children when problems arose!

EDITORS' REFLECTIONS BOX 2: LOOKING BENEATH THE SURFACE AT PEER INTERACTION

We think Lisa's observation extract in the previous section could easily be understood as 'friendly rivalry' between these three children. However, another way of understanding it is that it demonstrates the children's need to feel 'superior' to the rest of the group. The children compete with each other to demonstrate their skills and prowess. The rest of the group apparently admired these qualities, and the group of three were 'popular'.

When Lisa talked about the children's play in the Work Discussion group, the group discussion focussed on issues of power. We talked about how the three children acted as a gang, teasing, inviting other children to join them, and then excluding them.

This raised questions in the Work Discussion group about what might be going on at home to make the three feel so vulnerable. We wondered if what was going on was a very common way of how children attempt to get rid of their own negative feelings. They 'put' those feelings into another child by making that child feel those feelings. In this example, Mary is making Rik feel 'resigned and sad' so that she, Mary, does not have to have to feel these painful feelings. Instead, Mary can feel powerful and enjoy that feeling instead.

Rik seemed a little different, though, from the other two, bullying much less than Mary. Lisa says at the end of her observation that Rik had noticed Lisa observing James. The Work Discussion group wondered if maybe Rik was relieved that Lisa had observed the group dynamics and had cottoned on, that is, had understood what was going on.

It might be helpful to nursery staff, who want to encourage friendly and supportive relationships between young children, to think about what may have been going on here beneath the surface.

Observation supporting pedagogy, observation as pedagogy!

Observing children in this way, that is, including attention to children's emotional experiences, can a have a powerful and positive impact on our pedagogy. Our knowledge of individual children and of childhood is strengthened. Because our full attention is on the child, as well as our own emotional responses to what we are seeing, the whole observation becomes imprinted in our memory. I can still remember the detail of 'Tavistock observations' (see Chapter 7) that I carried out five years ago. You are not interrupted by writing things down, taking photos or thinking about 'assessments'. You feel you have experienced what the children were experiencing and so the observation become like a vivid memory.

This close observation supports our pedagogy and the way in which we understand children. What we have seen, we do not forget, so we are able to hold our knowledge of the child, their joys and needs, as well as their sadnesses and collapses, at the forefront of our minds. After carrying out this observation, all my future interactions with the three children were enhanced by my knowledge of the intricacies of their relationship. I know that the children felt my interest in their play. They noticed me noticing them. I could feel an unspoken two-way recognition and respect between us. It served as a reminder that what children really want and need from us is our interest and understanding.

EDITORS' REFLECTIONS BOX 3: EXPERIENCING SOMETHING OF WHAT THE CHILDREN EXPERIENCE

We think it is very important that Lisa has included the full range of children's feelings – not only their positive emotions but negative ones, too, for example, their angers, upsets and collapses. We see these negative feelings as an important part of children's lives, too, even as babies, that need recognising and responding to. It is painful to see another human being's sadness or distress, especially a young child. How can we support each other to see negative emotions, when they are there, as a matter of trying to understand everything that small children may need us to know about and respond to?

Work Discussion on Zoom rather than in a room

When Covid arrived, our Work Discussion sessions moved to online Zoom sessions. The work within my setting itself was even more difficult than before Covid. Just as an illustration, I struggled with how to manage social distancing which obviously is totally impossible with the youngest children. A young child had recently tested positive. If we had been looking after him, he would have potentially passed the infection on to staff and their families and vice-versa. I was not sure whether or not I would feel comfortable holding a baby, for their sake more than mine. I would find it difficult to ask this of practitioners for whom I was responsible.

It was at this point that the Work Discussion sessions took a difficult turn for me. The connection that the group had been starting to develop in the face-to-face meetings was suddenly lost. It was so hard to connect with people, both literally and emotionally, on Zoom. Internet connections would fail, but most significantly, I found that I could not pick up the emotional signals through a screen. The sessions were difficult. To give an example of a session, the Zoom connection was unusually problematic with people literally disappearing and losing connection. On one occasion, the Work Discussion participants were talking generally before one read out her observation. This general discussion was about two funerals that two members of the group had attended since the previous session. I could not gauge from the screen what anyone in the group was thinking or feeling. At one point, Tricia, another member of the Work Discussion group, appeared to get upset and left the room, disappearing from the screen. This was not acknowledged in any way by the Work Discussion group facilitators or by any members of the group, perhaps not even noticed by anyone, and I felt I needed to withdraw from the Work Discussion group and the project, and I wrote to the group facilitators and told them this.

Looking back at this now, I remember how taking the time to put into words why I wanted to withdraw from the research helped me to think about all of the aspects of my life and work that were challenging. I was forced to acknowledge the increased amount of pressure and stress I was under running Nursery Schools during a pandemic. I was made to verbalise the increased work stress and increased responsibilities of looking after vulnerable family members. To actually stop and acknowledge the emotional strain I was under, helped. Thinking about the amount of people who relied on me put my feelings of being overwhelmed into an understandable context.

I reconsidered my decision to leave the Work Discussion group and went on to share my feelings more openly with the group and this helped too. The direction of the sessions changed, and we began to share examples of our day. Hearing about the challenges that other leaders faced and coped with, both personal and professional, re-created a sense of belonging and connection with the group for me.

When you are in a leadership position, it is all too often seen as unprofessional to find things difficult. We have a perception that we may be seen as weak or not capable of doing our job. We do not often admit to our feelings or ask for help when we need it.

EDITORS' REFLECTIONS BOX 4: THE IMPORTANCE OF A SAFE SPACE FOR NURSERY PRACTITIONERS TO TALK ABOUT THEIR REAL FEELINGS ARISING FROM THEIR WORK

We think nursery work is intensely emotional work, as well as physical and intellectual. Nursery practitioners deal with and manage so many feelings, in the children and in themselves, during every nursery working day. Covid produced a unique and even more difficult context in which already difficult and stressful nursery work had to continue. Lisa has written very honestly earlier about her feelings, for herself and for Tricia, for example, when Tricia left the screen for a few minutes and then returned to the Zoom.

Thinking about this later as the facilitators of the Work Discussion group, we felt that we should have picked up the possibility that Tricia had left the Zoom briefly because she had been upset by the discussion of the funerals. When someone is upset in a group, it can be a fine judgement whether to ask about it openly within the whole group or whether to move on with the discussion so that if the individual is upset about something, they do not end up feeling even more upset or embarrassed. Making that judgement is much easier when face-to-face in a room than on Zoom. However, part of the role of Work Discussion facilitators is to make that judgement. They can then support a group in feeling it is a safe space in which professional matters that affect one personally, and vice-versa, can be discussed and thought about. Staying with the difficult, painful feelings of a practitioner is just as important as it is for a child who is upset or angry. Of course, practitioners are entitled to keep private and painful feelings private, and Work Discussion should not intrude. However, when a practitioner cannot help personal feelings affect their work, we think they are entitled to have some support in managing those feelings so that they do not spill out so much into the work with the children.

Lisa's writing illustrates powerfully how the boundary between the personal self and the professional self is a complex one. She draws out how that boundary needs a safe professional space where the reality of that boundary for everyone individually can be thought about in an atmosphere that is trusting.

Work Discussion as a roller-coaster ride

It is fair to say that my experience of the Work Discussion group went on a bit of a roller-coaster ride, up and down, reflective of the unpredictable times we were all living through. However, at the end of the ride, I was convinced of the momentous benefits that Work Discussion provides. First and foremost, by allowing us to see through the eyes of the children that we observe, developing a depth of knowledge that supports our interactions and practice. But just as significantly, it allows us to reflect on our own feelings, speaking openly with other professionals in a similar position to you who have the insight to understand. It provides an essential opportunity to stop, to reflect and to understand aspects that span both our professional and personal lives. Work Discussion is a beneficial tool, but it is so much more than that. It is a way of developing our pedagogy, a way of recognising and reflecting on the demands of our profession and a way of creating environments in which childhood exists. I would argue that this is not just something we can benefit from; it is something that we have a moral obligation to pursue.

Experiencing a Work Discussion group

Sam

Coming to Work Discussion from a long career passionately committed to nursery work

When I began my teaching degree over 30 years ago, I absolutely knew I wanted to teach in the early years and particularly in the nursery. I was then fortunate to do two teaching practices in one of London's 'Open-Air' nurseries, started by Dr. Susan Isaacs in the 1920s, with a long history of child-centred education and with incredibly knowledgeable and passionate staff. 'Open-Air nurseries' began with the McMillan sisters, Margaret and Rachel, in the early 1900s as a response to the desperate living conditions the sisters witnessed in South-East London as a result of the Industrial Revolution. They advocated for school meals, health clinics, and outdoor learning and play. They recognised the value to health of sunlight, exercise, and fresh air for young children.

Most of my career has been in the nursery, in various settings and countries. I have worked in my current primary school in inner city London for over a decade as nursery manager, and for more than a decade previously, I was the early years coordinator in the same school, teaching in the nursery and reception classes. The nursery has spaces for up to 52 children per session, aged from 2 to 4, although numbers were lower at the time we introduced 2-year-olds.

The offer to participate in the Work Discussion project made me feel excited at the prospect of having the opportunity to reflect on practice together with other professionals with more experience of 2-year-olds outside of my setting. In my initial meeting with Peter Elfer about the Work Discussion project, he emphasised the importance of thinking about feelings at work as part of the Work Discussion process. The mention of 'feelings' in relation to my work in this initial conversation was intriguing because in the current setup of nursery provision, the opportunity can almost never be created to discuss and reflect on our own feelings.

In my roles as manager and coordinator, I have often been in the role of 'coach' in supervisions and in encouraging reflection on practice in settings. However, this project seemed to offer an opportunity for me to experience professional reflection as a pedagogue alongside peers. I anticipated that we would likely untangle some 'knotty' issues together. I presumed we would have had similar experiences and

 DOI: 10.4324/b23247-14

assumed that others would exploit the opportunity to examine the emotional load and sometimes difficult feelings around our work. I envisaged an opportunity to learn by sharing what we found emotionally challenging, as well as joyous. Both the challenge and the joy of working in the early years is that one is constantly learning. Each new group of children has a unique dynamic, and every individual has the potential to offer a new perspective on how young children learn and respond.

Sharing the observation with the group

Part of my job is to hold the feelings of the children and their family members for them. These feelings can be overwhelming and cannot, therefore, be held or managed by the people to whom they belong. I then need to set my own feelings aside so that I can focus on those of the child and family and think about them carefully. In fact, my understanding of a 'professional' used to be of someone who largely ignored feelings and got on with the job. I was hoping, with this Work Discussion group, to explore my emerging doubts about this being the best way of managing at work. Possibly, this was one reason why I had chosen a complex interaction to share with the group.

EDITORS' REFLECTIONS BOX 1: BEING PROFESSIONAL AND DEALING WITH FEELINGS

We think Sam has made an important point earlier about what it means to be a *professional practitioner* in the early years and how to manage all the emotions one feels throughout each workday. Young children are brimming with feelings, and these can spill out all over the place. Parents, too, may have a lot of feelings about letting their child go and trusting the nursery practitioners. Practitioners will pick up these feelings and are bound to have their own emotional responses to them. These 'work feelings' can sometimes become mixed up with feelings that originate outside the nursery. Nursery practitioners may have had drummed into them that they should not express their feelings at work, especially negative ones! That is quite right. It would be unprofessional to let out one's feelings in front of children, parents, or colleagues. However, that does not mean that it is professional to pretend not to have any feelings! A nursery practitioner could not do their job without having feelings. And they could not be responsive to children, without being open to their feelings too. Work Discussion, away from the children and families, is a space where the feelings stirred up through the work, the joyous ones, and the challenging ones, can be acknowledged, shared, and thought about together. When this can happen, it is much less likely that a negative feeling will come across to a child or parent or colleague, even though the practitioner may be trying to 'hide it'. So being professional, we would say, means the capacity to bear all the feelings stirred up in a situation, holding onto them, but setting them to one side to address later. This can then be done in a professional reflection forum like Work Discussion, away from the frontline work, where there is time and space to talk and think about the emotional dynamics of the child and family and how the practitioner may have been affected by these.

I was the first to present an observation of a child for discussion to our group in a series of 12 fortnightly discussion sessions, and I had not yet formed relationships or built trust within the group. It is possibly because of this that I found the process of presenting to be very emotionally challenging. This was partly because it was an uncomfortable observation of a 2-year-old and his mother struggling to separate from each other. It was uncomfortable at that time, in the write up, and to share with the group. It was also challenging for me to share because I was exposing my and my colleagues' work from our setting. Inevitably, I have strong feelings of loyalty to my workplace. In a discussion about practice in one's own setting, it is easy to feel criticised, and I did take some comments personally.

My presentation was about David. David was almost 2-and-a-half years old.

David had been attending for around five months from soon after his second birthday, although his attendance was very sporadic. The Key Person and I had had many conversations with the mother around settling and the importance of regular routines and attendance. By her own admission, although Mum was reluctant to bring David to nursery and struggled with the feeling of 'letting him go', she also felt that it was 'right' for David to come. His mother stated that David needed more challenge and stimulation than she could provide at home. In other words, Mother clearly had mixed feelings about David attending nursery. Rationally, she felt it was the right place for David, but underneath, emotionally, she could not really bear the thought of letting him go.

> Crying David, (real, wet tears), is handed to the Key Person from his mother's arms, with the Key Person saying lots of reassuring, greeting welcomes in sing-song tones. With his mouth open, David looks along his outstretched arm, fist opening and closing, toward departing Mum.
>
> 'Shall we have a story?', asks the Key Person, 'you love a story, David' as David spins his head to be able to see the door. The Key Person carries a now quietly crying David to a comfy chair, scooping up a book from a selection on the table and settles David onto her lap, back-to-chest, arms wrapped around him, with the book out in front. David sniffles but has stopped crying and is looking at the book. He still has his jacket on and I'm aware that I think, 'he's not stopping!' meaning I perceive the child to think he doesn't want to commit to staying, or similar. David appears interested in the book – he is calmer, still looking at it for a while until he suddenly says 'Mummy . . .' and indicates the direction of the door, with his face and hand. The Key Person interpreted, as I would have done, that communication meaning 'I want to go back to the door' and the Key Person responds by getting up and placing David on the floor. He glances up at the Key Person and they head towards the door. I am pleased that it seems a familiar routine to both, directed by the child.
>
> As they go past the play dough table, the Key Person says, 'Playdough? You love the playdough David! Shall we play with the playdough?' David accepts the released hand without reaction but watches the Key Person closely as she

sits as if to be certain she is going to sit with him. Possibly once reassured of this, he changes his glance and looks towards the dough. Although invited to sit, he chooses to stand, and gazes at what seemed to be nothing in particular, like a daydream. He starts to play, very tentatively, with the backs of his fingers at first, then gently turns them over and softly taps the dough. (The observation continues describing David's increasing engagement with the playdough.)

Thus, the observation extract above, taken from the observation narrative, that was shared with the group, was one of a crying child being handed to his Key Person by his mother and the upset child's slow settling-in to the session.

I knew that there had been very many sessions where David's mother had stayed initially but that had not necessarily supported the child to explore the environment and 'move away' from his mother. So then the next stage of settling had taken place, where David's mother had left for ever-increasing amounts of time, starting with just a few minutes to reassure the child that although Mummy goes, she returns very quickly. David would respond very well and then be absent for a few days, and settling would have to begin all over again.

David was usually fine after 5–10 minutes and would go off and play independently and, at times, could often be seen dancing and skipping or in play alongside peers. At that time, I was confident that he was competently being supported both physically and emotionally by a familiar adult who had good knowledge of the child and context. Afterwards, through the Work Discussion group and in discussions with the facilitators, I began to feel that if we had been able to work more with David's mother, helping her understand how torn she felt between her desire for David to come to nursery and wanting to keep David at home, we may have been able to move the situation forward more effectively. Of course, we did tell the mother that David did settle, but it needed more than 'telling' and needed a piece of work to demonstrate to mother that we recognised and understood her mixed feelings about David being in nursery. Unfortunately, we do not always have the time or skills or authority to do this kind of work.

I began to feel that if we had had a Work Discussion process earlier, or even while we were settling David, we might have understood why all the support we were giving the mother was not actually helping with the nub of the problem – that is, her mixed feelings about leaving her son.

EDITORS' REFLECTIONS BOX 2: PUTTING PAINFUL FEELINGS INTO WORDS

We can see from the observation, and know from Sam, how hard David's Key Person is trying to settle David and how Sam, as observer, feels David was completely supported, and in a way, David was. It can be very painful to see this when a child is clearly distressed and unhappy at the transition into nursery and when nursery practitioners are working so hard to offer a warm and welcoming environment. Everyone naturally wishes the distress and unhappiness could be avoided. Perhaps the Key Person allowing David to lead her to the door through which Mummy departed is an example of this. We wonder, though, if this might have been confusing for David, who might have thought that he was going to be allowed to go home.

Drawing on our experience of working with a wide range of nurseries, we know from practitioners how much pressure there can be to stop a child being openly upset at transition times. We know it can be very tempting to try and distract the child from their upset by quickly encouraging them to take up, or join in, an activity.

We also know from Sam that the practitioners really had previously tried many, many times to explore emotions with David and to acknowledge and validate them, including using 'social stories', but he was still upset. In the end, some distraction was used, as happens in so many nurseries, and indeed, families.

In general, when a practitioner can try and express in words what they think the child may be feeling at that time, as Sam said David's Key Person did, it can help the child feel the practitioner understands the cause of the child's distress. For example, the practitioner might say: 'I can see that you want to go home with Mummy, but your place today is at nursery, and we are going to have a nice time together until Mummy comes back later after tea'.

Using words (and sometimes touch and visuals too) in this way also helps the child put words to their own feelings. This helps the child to be able to communicate their feelings themselves and, in time, to be able to think about their feelings and the feelings of others.

The challenge when parents are ambivalent about their child coming to nursery

The ambivalence of the mother in this situation was possibly being projected[1] *into* the child. Whilst we have settling policies and procedures, sometimes we are greeted with challenging family dynamics. These then require support in a more individualised way through the settling process. These are the decisions we make as professionals every day in a range of situations, and these are the emotional demands placed on staff – sometimes trying to mediate between the needs of the child and the demands on the family in terms of work and other pressures. In this case, the mother's own hesitation and conflict; the level of control the child is able to have in the family at home and the way their relationship played out in the settling illustrates the way in which the settling process is not always easy and straightforward, and this can result in uncertainty among staff members as to whether or not they are doing the 'right thing'. There are intricate family emotional dynamics at play, and the ramifications reverberate into the setting. Yet as professionals, we are expected to 'fix' these emotion dilemmas with our policies and procedures. It is also expected that these situations do not have an impact on us, when, of course, they do.

EDITORS' REFLECTIONS BOX 3: FAMILIES FEELING AMBIVALENT

We think it is understandable to feel ambivalent about taking your child to nursery. In current times, most parents rely on help from outside the family to balance employment, parenting, and family life. Nursery can be so helpful and supportive to families as well as nurturing for children. Many parents know and value this but may still wish they could have more time to spend with their child and sometimes feel guilty that they're asking other people to look after their child. Although children may love going to nursery, the time of separation can be painful. In discussions, Sam had commented to us how difficult it was for some parents to commit to the process of settling into nursery and trust that their child would settle. We saw this as showing how Sam understands the obstacle that's getting in the way of allowing her child to settle: Mother's mixed feelings (her feelings of both wanting and not wanting David to come to nursery – that is, her ambivalence).

We also think Sam makes another important point. She had talked about the emotional demands placed on staff trying to juggle between the needs of the child and the needs of the family. We know that nurseries are intensely busy places, where staff are called upon to do an extremely difficult job. As Sam says, there is bound to be uncertainty sometimes in staff about whether or not they are doing the 'right thing'. That is why we think Work Discussion is so important as a place where practitioners can think about these complex feelings together without competition, judgement, or any sense of blame.

The feedback and discussion process: courage and exposure in honest professional reflection

The process of sharing your practice in a group opens you to the risk of feeling judged or sometimes of others in the group being judgemental. This can happen in their responses to your principles, practice, actions, and interpretation of situations. However, the purpose of Work Discussion is NOT to *judge* others but to *understand better* the actions and powerful emotions that occur in nursery work. Although we are professionals, we can have moments of uncertainty about the best way of dealing with tricky situations. Gaining a better understanding through professional reflection involves being prepared to acknowledge uncertainty so that we can be open to new ways of thinking about situations. This process of deep thinking exposes you to the risk of feeling judged or criticised by those who do not yet understand the processes of professional reflection. Yet real professional thinking requires us to sometimes move away from always being certain and to allow ourselves to be uncertain.

As participants, we were encouraged to be respectful to each other. It takes time for a group to learn about the possible upsetting impact of sharing their thoughts and reflections in response to the situation another member of the group has presented.

Sharing with peers from a range of settings means that there is not necessarily the same shared understanding of context as there would be from a Work Discussion group with colleagues in your own, or a familiar, setting. On the other hand, a Work Discussion group with your own colleagues holds risks too. Sometimes it is not so easy to see how the practices of your own setting are working for children and families because you are so familiar with them. Another risk is that colleagues may not always say what they really think because they do not want to risk upsetting others in their team setting with whom they work each day and whom they like and respect.

There is no 'one-size-fits-all' when it comes to supporting young children and their families to settle into nursery life. 'One-size-fits-all' demonstrates a reliance on policies and procedures rather than a consideration of the individual difficulties and conflicts that inevitably arise in any working situation.

This scenario highlights the often-present tensions between ideals and reality. Ideally, children will have been prepared emotionally for separation and nursery by the family, parents, or carers, and they would support them with regular attendance and commitment, but it is often far messier than that since these are real people with real lives and emotions. That is perhaps why Work Discussion matters so much in order to have a safe space (but not so safe as to avoid questioning anything) where some of this messy daily reality can be thought through with trusted others. This needs to happen in a spirit that is not competitive and where there is understanding that there are not necessarily right answers or the resources to do what may be needed.

The Work Discussion group (and the process of this writing) has given me the opportunity to reflect on the complexities of these relationships and their significance to the life of a young child. I had thought our responses were professional, caring, responsive, and based in much experience. However, what is also meeting here is not just a family and a setting but also a whole web of relationships with professional colleagues. These relationships will be different from one another and have different levels of trust. It is also an encounter between the approaches and practices of the nursery and those of the family. This is the reality of what we experience regularly in practice. The web of trust may be as delicate as a spider's web – carefully built and expanded and potentially easily broken.

The painfulness of seeing more clearly

> the pain of seeing clearly is . . . balanced by the pleasure of new insights into human relationships.
>
> (Reid, 1997, p. 3)

Sue Reid, in her book *Developments in Infant Observation: The Tavistock Model*, talks about the Tavistock model of observing (see Chapter 7 for more information on the model) and describes how difficult it can be to observe in this way, seeing and feeling the painful emotions young children sometimes have alongside their joyful experiences. Yet she makes clear that if a group of professionals can be brave enough to hear about these painful emotions and talk about them, it may bring benefits to children and practitioners:

At the time of discussing with the Work Discussion group David's settling into nursery, I did indeed find the process very painful. As I have said earlier, comments on one's practice and that of one's colleagues can feel undermining and very much like unfair criticism, especially when we consider the power of one's feelings of strong loyalty to one's work setting and colleagues. We absolutely make our best endeavors in ever more challenging contexts. Most of the time, we are satisfied that our efforts are making a difference and having an impact. I do not think we could do the job otherwise. However, there can be times when we wish we could do more if only we had more resources. I was left wondering if we had got it wrong for David. I began to have some doubts about elements of my practice. Looking at the Work Discussion experience now and my painful memories of discussing this difficult family situation, with the perspective of the confident and happy David (who had left us for a term, only to return), there is a very different feeling. The confident child who returned linked closely with the little David, 'dancing and skipping, or in play alongside his peers', whom we used to see in the nursery. It was clearly the actual separation and settling each day that was so difficult for David. The obvious implication was that our work with David had had a much greater positive impact than I had feared.

Knowing how painful and unsettling the Work Discussion process can be, I may have been more guarded and less likely to be as vulnerable had I not been the first to present. But then the potential value of Work Discussion for creating new learning and increasing awareness of the psychological pressures of the work at times would be lost and that would be more than unfortunate. Exactly as Sue Reid says, seeing and learning can be painful, but if we can find the courage to share observations honestly, there can be real benefits for our pedagogy and for children and families. A difficult experience of a Work Discussion group could mean that other members of the group then avoid sharing observations openly, in effect 'censoring' their presentations and choosing less challenging subject matter or 'easier' children to discuss. This would reduce the potential of the group to support all children in a range of situations or create hypotheses about patterns of behaviour which are confusing or disturbing. That would be such a loss of the opportunity to think more deeply about our practice. Each individual group member will decide for themselves 'whether the pain of seeing clearly is sufficiently balanced by the pleasure of new insights into human relationships' (Reid, 1997, p. 3).

EDITORS' REFLECTIONS BOX 4: THE COURAGE TO SEE PEDAGOGICAL RELATIONSHIPS CLEARLY AND OUR PART IN THEM

We think Sam was very brave to offer to be first to present in the Work Discussion group, describing the situation of David and his mother struggling to settle in at nursery. She was honest about the careful work she and her colleagues had done and about the feeling that all this work had not so far enabled David to settle and enjoy all that the nursery had to offer. She has done the valuable job here of vividly illustrating Work Discussion as a place to think about the nitty-gritty of the daily work with children and families and the individual feelings that can get stirred up in us by that work. She has shown how real professional reflection is more than just patting each other on the back. It is about thinking honestly about complex emotional dynamics in early years work, which is so often seen from outside as easy and uncomplicated work. We think practitioners who can do this, sometimes painful, real reflection, are working at a much more sophisticated and engaged level than practitioners who claim that they leave any personal feelings at the nursery door.

Anyone might understandably think that it would feel better to discuss a difficult nursery interaction with a group of peers who merely praised and congratulated you on all your efforts. However much that may feel safer and more rewarding in a temporary way, it is not what Work Discussion is all about. We think, too, that practitioners might prefer to face the painful feelings of dealing with uncertainty and struggling with new thinking, enabling them to learn a deeper pedagogical practice, than simply carry on with the same old ways of working.

The potential value of Work Discussion

Our Work Discussion group was a temporary, short-term, time-defined project which has a different level of investment and commitment than one's daily professional team. It was further complicated by the need to switch to remote meetings due to Covid 'lockdown' which members reported had an impact on their ability to feel part of a group through 'Zoom'.

I concluded from my experience that the dynamic of the group is crucial to the success of a Work Discussion group because exploring the emotions of infants, toddlers, or children, along with their families, will not always be easy or comfortable. Therefore, the group must be cohesive, and it takes time to develop this. Groups need to develop trust and 'openness' to the process and be willing to be vulnerable and exposed. This inevitably is part of the role of the Work Discussion group facilitators.

Although I found the presentation very difficult and emotionally exhausting, I still believe Work Discussion groups offer huge opportunity to increase our understanding of some of the youngest children in society and to improve practice through increased perception and awareness. There is a different level of intensity to this method, an increased attentiveness. We are looking for, and at, emotion, and Work Discussion gives 'permission' to acknowledge our own emotions as they arise from, and influence, our work with children and families.

Since participating in the project, I am more likely to observe without taking notes, to be 'in the moment', and to be more aware of thinking about the internal world of the child. This has been particularly useful with our 2-year-olds, who may be less verbal, or with our non-verbal children of all ages.

Work Discussion groups are not about judgement or showcasing best practice; they are about the real-world, day-to-day realities of lived experiences, and the Work Discussion group participants need to feel able to share all aspects of their thoughts and responses. Some may find this easier than others. The question then becomes, would we be brave enough to bring our most vulnerable selves, with difficult observations, or would we 'play safe'? Are we confident enough to recognise that we may not know everything? Are we so entrenched in the practice and culture of our own setting that it may be difficult to listen to another perspective or approach?

For the children, the benefits could be better relationships with staff who are more equipped and supported to tune in to each child's personality and emotional needs and support their skills and efforts as social and emotional individuals. As reflective practitioners, we hope that we start with the child and build an environment to support their needs. Observation need not only be used for assessment. In the current educational culture of 'measurement', we need a reminder to observe in order to really recognise even the most subtle of responses from the child. This will enable us to improve relationships with young children through better understanding.

Note

1 The term 'projection' is discussed in Chapter 2.

12 Experiencing a Work Discussion group

Tricia

Professional background

I have been working in early years for around 20 years, currently as Deputy Manager of a preschool setting. I originally trained as a Montessori teacher and enjoyed the course but wanted to explore the pedagogies of other pioneers and became interested in the work of Friedrich Froebel. I was particularly struck by his idea of children being able to grow and develop at their own pace, viewed from the child's perspective, not the adult's. I love the fact that Froebel encourages the idea of children being active in their own learning and that play is the most appropriate way for them to learn. He advocated for the adult to be a sensitive guide and support for the children to have the confidence to pursue their own interests, and this has linked very strongly with my own pedagogy of developing strong emotional connections with children.

I joined the pilot scheme for what was then known as Early Years Professional Status, now referred to as Early Years Teacher Status (EYTS). The pilot scheme had hoped to bring parity between practitioners and teachers' status and conditions of service. I found it hugely frustrating and disappointing that this was not achieved. However, my desire to lead practice and share knowledge and experiences remained. This led me to gain a Masters in Early Childhood (MAEC). Part of my role as Deputy Manager of the preschool is to mentor and support staff and run training for parents and practitioners. I also teach the Early Years Foundation degree, BA top-up degree, and Level 3 (NVQ) in a local college.

Encountering Work Discussion

Part of my MAEC study was discussing our own observations of children under three, and this included attention to emotional experience. The module inspired me to develop my interest in emotional connections with children and how they can be thought about within a group of practitioners. However, there is a big difference between enjoying talking about the positive things young children have accomplished and opening up in a group to colleagues, talking about the more difficult parts of interactions with children, family members, and sometimes with

DOI: 10.4324/b23247-15

colleagues. This is how I came to understand what Work Discussion was all about. It is about being part of a group, always with the same members, always with a trained facilitator. You have to be prepared to describe how individual children make you feel and express those individual feelings and responses in different pedagogic interactions. This is not easy, especially where there are difficulties or dilemmas. You listen to the reflections of others in the group, trusting each other's thought and opinions, so that you can think about your own practice in a deeper but always constructive way. The opportunity, therefore, to learn about Work Discussion as a form of professional reflection, and to participate in a Work Discussion group, was something I wanted to do. The space to try and make sense, with trusted colleagues in a group, of the uncertainties or complexities that we can all encounter in our day-to-day work is very important to me.

From meeting face-to-face to talking on Zoom

Whilst the first four sessions of our Work Discussion group were together, face-to-face in a room, our meetings had to change to being on Zoom due to the Covid emergency and the national lockdown. It was a time when everything changed for all of us. I am aware that some of my colleagues in the Work Discussion group found having to go to Zoom sessions as lockdown became a reality very challenging but I enjoyed it. The travelling to the Work Discussion meetings was time-consuming and exhausting. I very much wanted to be a part of the group, and being able to continue with the group via Zoom made life easier for me in practical terms.

With students, I found I got used to teaching remotely, but it was also a real barrier to connecting with my students. As teenagers, they sometimes need as much personal and social support as our youngest children. I know I thrive on that emotional connection. It is a big part of my working life in early years, something I feel strongly about, so perhaps it's as much about my loss as theirs.

However, moving to meeting remotely for our Work Discussions, I did not feel too much of a disconnect with the other members of the group. I felt we were able to create relationships with each other due to the sessions together before lockdown. I found the group to be a very supportive place, professionally, whilst going through the very frightening experience of Covid.

EDITORS' REFLECTIONS BOX 1: RELATIONSHIP CONNECTIONS AND INTERNET CONNECTIONS

We think Tricia's comments about 'connections' with other members of the group raises an interesting point. There are two types of 'connection' when meeting on Zoom: 'connection' in the sense of the strength of relationships with others in the group (a relational connection) and 'connection' in the physical internet connection sense.

The first case raises the question of whether or not you can feel the same depth of 'relational connection' to someone on Zoom as you can when sitting next to them in a room and how can you build that online?

If participants are going to really reflect with depth and honesty on the details of their work with children, families, and other practitioners, there needs to be a sense of trust and safety in the group. It means building 'connections' with each other where you can speak honestly about your work. No one wants to end up feeling judged, or criticised, or told, 'This is what you should do!' When an interaction with a child or family is not going well, ALL the participants in that interaction, including the practitioner, must ask, 'Is there something I am doing that may not be helping?' Others can often see that more clearly that we can ourselves. Being open to hearing what others have to say about our work takes courage!

There is also the reality of our 'physical connections' together. In one of the sessions, we experienced a major internet outage so that we all lost connections to each other. There were other shorter interruptions to our connection together. And taking turns to talk without talking over one another is trickier on Zoom than when together. Most readers will have experienced this at some time. You will know how disruptive and frustrating it can feel, especially if it happens at a sensitive time. Online working can be exhausting, even without all the other obstacles that practitioners must overcome. Is there a way, though, of using this experience, so frustrating for us as adults, to think about the experience of young children in nursery? It can so easily happen that practitioners are interrupted in the middle of an interaction with a child – needing to attend urgently to something else.

Children clearly feel an even greater sense of sudden disconnection, and the frustration and abandonment that can follow, than us as adults.

Work and Work Discussion during Covid

Some members of the group said they found the process of being on Zoom challenging, and it felt almost intimidating having everyone look at you as you spoke. I did not notice this feeling or sense of intimidation, although it could be very frustrating when people interrupted each other or spoke over one another – something that is not always easy to avoid on Zoom. It is inevitable, though, that different members of the Work Discussion group experienced the group differently at different times. I describe later a time in the group when we were talking about an experience of attending a funeral. This touched on my own personal experience, and I could feel myself becoming extremely upset. It shows how experiences from outside our work can affect our work. As professionals, we manage that ourselves most of the time, but sometimes, we need some help too. Having an upsetting or confusing experience is one thing. Talking about it to understand it and manage it better can be upsetting and confusing too. Work Discussion is one place where than can happen.

There were times during Covid when I could feel terrified about going into work, really frightened. What I found particularly beneficial for me is the fact that during our discussions, we knew that everyone involved was having similar experiences, as we came from the same profession. We were able to understand the difficulties and frustrations we all had not just in terms of the pandemic but also the lack of support and guidance from the government and then the shocking and distressing media backlash towards the teaching profession. We shared the reality of all our situations which was why we could reassure each other. We had the immense responsibility of keeping children safe, of enabling them to feel secure, and of keeping ourselves and our colleagues safe. It was an extremely worrying and stressful situation, and we were almost being vilified. How we felt about this and our own personal experiences or personal losses were pushed to the side. We had to focus on the children, their families, and for me, my students. The media backlash and government disregard was one of the most difficult experiences I had during lockdown. I valued being able to share this with each other in the group discussions.

There was a three-week gap between finishing our face-to-face meetings and the first meeting on Zoom. It was in this meeting that I read my observation of Harriet. Here is a brief description of Harriet:

> Harriet was four years when I observed her for the Work Discussion group. She is a girl who feels things so deeply. Harriet had had contact with the Pre-School before starting so she was a little familiar with us staff and she knew me. It was the year that she started that her family experienced some difficulties. Harriet would go from 0–100 in no time with real meltdowns and a huge sense of rage. She would then be very upset about how angry she had been. I could spot the triggers. I found that the key thing was to get down to her level. I never told her to calm down. I know that is pointless when a child is that angry. I try to put her feelings into words, to give her the words to use so that she can try and tell me what she feels and so that we can talk about it afterwards.

When I presented my observation of Harriet, I was the first one of the group to proo ent via Zoom. This was a challenge that I enjoyed. But I had other feelings too. The observation I had prepared was written a few weeks before lockdown, and speaking about Harriet, I felt very emotional, as I considered the possibility that I may not see her again before she left preschool and would be starting in reception from September. We had no clear idea of when lockdown would end nor the implications of such a complete lockdown. I was also conscious of the fact that children can come to mean so much to you as a practitioner. It was the experience of 'Professional Love' that Jools Page has discussed and that we have for the children (for more about 'Professional Love', see the editorial comments box later). I considered that I may end up feeling quite protective of Harriet as the group discussed her.

In the observation, I wrote about Harriet's Key Person and how she talked with her about cutting up fruit:

> I watched as Harriet was cutting a pear. She said 'I can't do it, I'm not strong enough!'. Her Key Person responded, 'yes you are, look, cut it like a saw'. She demonstrated on the pear and gave the knife back to Harriet. She cut the pear 'Is that too big?' she asked. 'Yes, I think it is, maybe cut it a little more'. Harriet continued cutting the pear. She concentrated and was focussed on the task. I realised she had not made any attempt to engage me in conversation or show me what she was doing. I hadn't expected that. I realised that I was feeling a little put out! She was calm and enjoying the task and did not need any reassurance or support from me.

EDITORS' REFLECTIONS BOX 2: PERSONAL FEELING IN PROFESS-IONAL RELATIONSHIPS

We think this reference to Tricia's feelings in relation to Harriet is a good example of an aspect of a professional relationship with a child. Tricia includes some of the personal feelings that relationship may evoke in the practitioner that it is so important to talk about in Work Discussion. Here, she talks about 'feeling a little put out', a perfectly understandable and ordinary human emotion! It is also a good example of the courage practitioners need to talk about their relationships with children so that they are open to discussion and comment from others in the Work Discussion group. Jools Page, the academic, who also used to be a Nursery Leader, is the person who developed the concept of 'Professional Love' in early years settings. She describes its meanings and limits in many publications. We think it will be very helpful for readers of this book to also read Jools's work so they can deepen their understanding of the meaning of 'Professional Love' (Page, Clare and Nutbrown, 2013). It is not an easy aspect of professional relationships to talk about because it could be so easily confused with something as inappropriate and unprofessional. 'Professional Love' is all about how the emotional needs of the child always are the first consideration. We think Tricia's reference to how much Harriet matters to her and her feeling put out by Harriet's apparent independence from her are highly professional of her to share. It allows the Work Discussion participants to support Tricia in thinking about her professional relationship with Harriet so that the close relationship she has built with her is always focussed on her needs and wellbeing.

Some members of the group were not able to provide observations, as their settings were closed during Covid. I was able to continue working, as restrictions eased in June 2020 and we opened to more children and I was required at preschool. I undertook a second observation, as I wanted to discover if lockdown had any effect on Harriet.

- Had her behaviour changed in any way?
- Was she showing signs of distress or anxiety?
- How was she coping with our new routines and less resources?

I also wondered about my own anxiety being amongst people and whether adapting from lockdown would have had any effect on Harriet.

Would she pick up on my anxiety and react to it?

I found it fascinating that the children all coped remarkably well with coming back into the preschool setting. It actually settled my nerves and concerns very well, as we just got back into the swing of things together. Harriet adapted well, she did not seem concerned that there were less resources available, and we never heard a child mention they were bored. I feel the relationships we had developed before lockdown were so strong that the children felt safe and secure in the setting and so were able to make the best use of the resources and found joy in being back together.

Work Discussion as a place to include emotions in pedagogical reflection

Early years practitioners are taught, quite rightly, not to allow their feelings to influence their observations and their judgements. All too often as I have explained, we have to keep our feelings and emotions to ourselves. I have described it as putting on a show: Once the children arrive, I am no longer Tricia. I am a professional person, putting all my concerns to one side. But is it really as straightforward as this?

Like many people during the awful pandemic, I lost a family member who became unwell and died without us seeing her or being with her. She was a hugely important person in my life, always on my side and my greatest fan. She was a friend, someone I loved to spend time with. I was blessed to have her in my life for so many years, and losing her was devastating.

One of the participants in our Work Discussion group had attended an online funeral and was discussing this at the start of one of our Zoom sessions. Although able to attend the funeral of the family member I had lost, it meant a four-hour journey there and back for a 15 minute funeral. There were no flowers, and I was not able to comfort members of my family and I was dreading it. As my colleague talked about the online funeral in the Work Discussion group, I just could not cope with it. The very last thing I needed or wanted was to talk about a funeral, but it seemed important to her to share her experiences. Eventually, I asked if we could please stop talking about funerals, as I was becoming extremely upset. I was aware that this was a professional Work Discussion group, and I was embarrassed to be emotional. It did not feel appropriate, and I excused myself, leaving the Zoom briefly, to gather myself.

The Work Discussion session started, and I rejoined as quickly as I could. No one acknowledged what had happened. No one in this Zoom meeting asked me if I was ok. One participant sent me a text to check how I was. Letting my own emotions show and talking about what was happening in my personal life did not feel like the right or professional thing to do. I think this is something as practitioners we do struggle with because we sometimes do need to acknowledge things that happen to us outside of work since they do affect us in how we work and we may feel that having personal feelings conflicts with the desire to remain professional. I feel it is natural as humans to wish for some comfort, and perhaps some acknowledgement of my distress may have been helpful, just to know it was noticed and supported in a small way. Much in the same way as I behave when I'm working with the children or my students, we are there for them to support them. However, our own feelings, our emotions do not seem to be given any importance or relevance. We are supposed to leave all that at the nursery door. I have always believed this. I understood that my leaving the discussion briefly was not addressed; I have at no point in this pandemic been asked at college how I am coping. I did not discuss with them my deep distress at my own bereavement or the fact that I have not been able to see my mum now for a year. How we as teachers are coping with our own feelings and emotions during this crisis or since the crisis, has, I feel, been ignored. Our emotions do not seem to be particularly valued in education, and in the fight to show that in the early years, we are professionals, not just babysitters, I believe I try too hard to leave all my personal worries and anxieties at the door.

EDITORS' REFLECTIONS BOX 3: HUMANS OR ROBOTS IN THE WORKFORCE?

Feelings are important in the work. We have said before that we would never want robots working with small children! It is the humanity and empathy of practitioners that matter so much. So when we talk about leaving feelings at the door, this is not quite what we mean. Is it more that we need to have the ability to KNOW about what our real feelings are (not what we would like our feelings to be!) and the ability to THINK about those feelings? The fact that practitioners are human beings with feelings like any other human being does not make them any less professional. Surely, it is much more professional and important to acknowledge feelings so that it is then possible to think about their impact on work relationships with colleagues and children and families than pretending practitioners do not have feelings in the workplace and that they are all left at the nursery door. This is NOT to say that nursery is a place where practitioners can be talking about their feelings at any time in a way that is more focussed on them as practitioners than on the children. Major feelings that are preventing a practitioner from working effectively need to be discussed in private with more senior staff. But feelings in general, both positive and negative, are an inevitable and vital part of work with young children, and they need a regular and special space (Work Discussion) in which their contribution and influence can be thought about. This is exactly what Tricia was beginning to do when she brought the Work Discussion group's attention to the different feelings she had in relation to Harriet, feeling protective of her in the discussion and feeling 'put out' that she did not seem to need her help in cutting her fruit.

Practitioners 'observing themselves' as they establish deeper relationships with children

A key interest I have in my profession is the connection that we make with the children in our care. How vital that is to their sense of wellbeing! But the environment must be right for this to occur. Practitioners need time to establish deeper relationships with the children and support to understand their own feelings. Introducing Work Discussion groups into our practice, I feel, could be an opportunity to explore these connections and how they affect us. This could give more experienced staff a chance to establish an environment of nurturing and mentoring each other. For example, being able to discuss the distress of attending the funeral I described earlier, during a time of a national pandemic, would have been helpful, as I was grieving so deeply. I am sure that had some effect on my behaviour, and being able to explain this could have been useful for me in enabling me to understand it more. This feels important to me, as we are a community-run preschool. We recently celebrated how long we have been open, and many former pupils came to celebrate with us, including a grandmother whose own children went to preschool and now their children do. This demonstrates the connections we make and the value we have in our community and in enabling staff to discuss the relationships they develop with the children and their families is critical in ensuring we continue to play a supportive role in our community. Working with young children evokes many emotions in us; the children have such a profound impact on us but only for a short period of time before they leave us and move on to school. These separations can feel brutal, really brutal. I wonder if as a profession, we do not like to make a big deal of things like our professional relationships. It is very hard that no one does make a big deal of early years work: 'It's only looking after small children'. So we complain that society does not make a big deal of working with other people's children, but I think we do not seem to want to make a big deal of it either. Maybe we are defensive as a profession. We are so used to be looking down upon, used, not valued, being only a number or part in a larger system. How do we get a sense of who we are, our agency, our importance? We form these strong bonds with the children, knowing they will end when the children move on and we will need to develop the same intense relationship with the next cohort.

EDITORS' REFLECTIONS BOX 4: PAIN AND LOSS IN EARLY CHILDHOOD PEDAGOGY

There is no doubt about the depth of joy many practitioners feel in their work. Here, though, Tricia reminds us of the presence of pain and loss too. In this last section of Tricia's account, she speaks of the deep relationships that are so important to offer to children. Such deep relationships, provided they are shaped by the needs of each child, bring great joy and satisfaction. But inevitably, this may involve loss and sadness, too, as children leave and move on. Is it fair to ask practitioners to do this with child after child, year after year, without a reliable space to reflect on the dynamics of these relationships between practitioners and children as they form, evolve, and come to an end?

PART FOUR
What is involved in leading a Work Discussion group?

Building space to talk and think

Some key tasks for Work Discussion facilitators

Ruth Seglow and Peter Elfer

In this chapter, we look at the following:

- Why you cannot learn to facilitate a Work Discussion group by reading about it in this chapter! The chapter is NOT a 'how-to-do-it' manual!

- How facilitating a Work Discussion group needs some experiential learning through first being a participant within a 'training group'.

- Five key tasks that we think are core to the role of facilitating a Work Discussion group. Each task Is illustrated with an example from our experience in Work Discussion groups with nursery practitioners and one or more questions to support your own reflections on managing the Task.

Introduction

In this last chapter of the book, we want to begin to show readers who may be interested in leading a Work Discussion group, perhaps in their own nursery, how they can go forward to prepare for this.

Leading a Work Discussion group is NOT something one can prepare for ONLY by reading about it in a book. Trying to prepare only by reading would be like trying to become a skilled nursery practitioner ready to lead a nursery team, without any practical experience of what the work involves.

Similarly, an essential part of the preparation for facilitating a Work Discussion group is to have first experienced being part of a 'training group' (by which we mean a group focussed on training to facilitate Work Discussion). This Chapter therefore lists five key tasks that we think any Work Discussion facilitator must manage.

We hope the Chapter, together with the experience of being a participant in a 'training group', will give the reader a sense of what may be involved in facilitating a Work Discussion group and the frame of mind and thinking that is needed to do this.

DOI: 10.4324/b23247-17

Below, you will find five 'tasks' which we think are essential for the facilitator of any Work Discussion group.

Task one: Enabling open-ended questioning and curiosity within the group

Illustration

Sometimes in a group, there will be a member who is inclined to give a quite concrete or definite answer to a question that another group member has asked or the group is mulling over. This can shut down the discussion. It is more helpful if this 'answer' is not taken as 'THE ANSWER' to whatever issue is being discussed but just one of a range of possibilities that encourages further curiosity and exploration of the question. Thus, when training to be a facilitator, one needs to encourage the group to keep open minds and consider a range of perspectives and approaches to a particular issue.

Definite answers are sometimes important and can *be/feel* reassuring. However, many issues in early years practice are complex, do not have a simple answer, and need open minds, willing to explore the question further or perhaps more deeply.

Points of reflection

1. Have you ever raised a work issue in a training or discussion group that you wanted to talk over but where someone responded as if there were only one answer?

2. Can you recall how that felt?

Task two: Helping each person in the group to feel listened to and their point considered

Illustration

Some years ago, we held a Work Discussion group for nursery room leaders. One member of the group seemed to us a rather naturally withdrawn person who did not say anything in our first few meetings. We worried that he would not be able to contribute at all. However, after four sessions, the group found itself bogged down, struggling with a difficult issue. This person made such an insightful contribution that it helped the group see the issue from a completely new perspective. He seemed to have been easily silenced by more 'confident' members of the group in the past, but this time, when another group member talked across him, we interrupted and invited the group to go back to listening to what he was saying.

Points of reflection

1. In work groups, would you say you tend to be a quieter participant or one who speaks quite a lot?

2. If the answer to the question depends on what kind of work group it is and who are the members, what would you say helps or hinders you speaking?

Task three: Keeping the focus on pedagogical interactions but recognising *and addressing of* the contribution of personal feelings within this

Illustration

An old wisdom we have often heard from senior nursery practitioners and leaders is that the professional practitioner leaves their personal feelings at the nursery front door. There is a lot in this wisdom. It would hardly be good practice if nursery practitioners were coming into nursery so distracted by their private lives that they could not fully attend to the children or their feelings were spilling out onto the children.

However, it is more complicated than a question of simply leaving all your feelings at the nursery front door! It is the warmth, empathy, passion, and commitment of nursery practitioners that is at the heart of effective pedagogy.

In a Work Discussion group, the Head of a nursery told us that one of her staff had come back to work after two weeks of compassionate leave following the death of her husband. The practitioner said she felt better out of the house. However, the Head said she did not think the practitioner had her mind on the children and often seemed 'absent'. The Head wondered what to do for the best.

Work Discussion is about the pedagogy! The example earlier may be an extreme one. Nursery practitioners are very good at managing their personal feelings at work. Nevertheless, practitioners, however much they claim they leave their personal feelings at the nursery door, will sometimes come in preoccupied by something that has happened outside of the nursery or, alternatively, inside the nursery. Practitioners are encountering the intense feelings of babies and young children all the time in their work. We think it is very demanding to manage these all the time in a professional way, without ever getting frustrated, angry, or overwhelmed. Practitioners must remain professional and in control when with the children. Work Discussion is a space where personal reactions, whether from within or outside the nursery, may need to temporarily become the focus of the group IN ORDER to allow everyone to return to focussing on the child or family being discussed.

Points of reflection

Although the expression of feeling is, of course, part of pedagogic work, can you think of a recent interaction where the personal feelings of a colleague have got in the way of what you have felt is the best pedagogic response to a child or adult?

1. If that interaction was discussed in a Work Discussion group, what might the group facilitator need to know or do to help the colleague and help the group think about it in a constructive way?

Task four: Working with the particular dynamics of a group, for example, silences, competitiveness, and defensiveness

Illustration

In a Work Discussion group of practitioners in a rather isolated, rural area, the nursery practitioners had been discussing the importance of the relationships made between the nursery and the families of children coming to the nursery. We had finished the discussion and come to a natural pause when one of the practitioners said, in an almost absent-minded way: 'Of course, you have your favourites'.

The rest of her team responded with a deafening silence. She looked embarrassed and said, 'Oh, come on, you guys. You know you have your favourites!'

The team were still silent until one said, in a rather grudging tone of voice: 'Well, I suppose deep down . . . but you would never let it show'.

The atmosphere in the group had suddenly changed from being relaxed and at ease to being tense and uneasy. The response of the practitioner who had first made the comment about 'favourites' was defensive and embarrassed. She seemed desperate for reassurance. It was very difficult to get the group to think about what she had said and share their own thoughts. Maybe the other participants had thought the one who had spoken meant it was acceptable to show favouritism if you felt it.

Our response as facilitators was to suggest to the group that this was an important issue to think about. However, the refusal to talk about it meant a silence in which the first practitioner seemed to become even more tense and anxious. We faced a dilemma. Should we wait to see if the group could find the courage to discuss this? Or should we move on to prevent the practitioner who had first spoken from feeling increasingly exposed and embarrassed?

We come back to these questions in Task five later.

Points of reflection

1. Can you recall being in a group where one person suddenly seems to be standing out for some reason, exposed and 'under the spotlight'?

2. How did the group leader and the group participants respond in this situation?

Task five: Ensuring a space for yourself, as facilitator, to receive support in thinking about and understanding your experience as facilitator

Illustration

In the Task four illustration earlier, we asked some questions about how the facilitators could have best helped this group of nursery practitioners to think together, in a supportive and uncritical way, about the issue of practitioners inevitably feeling differently towards different children and family members but of needing to act towards everyone with equal concern and attention.

The facilitators were faced with a group that was silent. It was as if the group had made an unconscious decision together that the topic was not one they were prepared to talk about. It is a good example of one type of group dynamic. There are many other examples of group dynamics:

A group may do the opposite of being silent, and all talk at once without anyone really listening to anyone else!

A group may become very competitive with one another, each implying that their way of thinking or working is 'best'.

A group may become defensive and avoid any thinking together about the issues within the group instead focussing attention on issues outside the group, about which they are not in any position to take any action.

A group may divide up into two or more factions, with each insisting that their point of view is the correct one and the other part of the group has got it wrong. The factions can then be focussed on 'winning' the argument rather than on trying to understand the differences in the group.

Silences, competitiveness, defensiveness, and other kinds of group dynamics are difficult for Work Discussion group facilitators to manage because they get in the way of constructive critical thinking.

We, therefore, think it is vital that facilitators have their own systems of adequate support. By this, we mean a regular opportunity for a facilitator to discuss, individually or as a member of a group themselves, together with a skilled and experienced facilitator in Work Discussion. This person needs to be someone who understands the complexities of talking and thinking in groups.

Points of reflection

1. Can you think of the advantages of this?
2. Can you think of disadvantages of this?
3. Can you think of examples of silence, of defensiveness, or of competitiveness within a group you have been in?
4. How was it managed?

Next steps

If you are interested in finding out more about training as a Work Discussion facilitator, please contact us on workdiscussion@gmail.com, and we would be pleased to talk this through with you and discuss training opportunities.

References

Azevedo, R. (2009) 'Theoretical, conceptual, methodological, and instructional issues in research on metacognition and self-regulated learning: A discussion', *Metacognition and Learning*, 4, pp. 87–95.

Brace, D. (2021) '"Settling In": Exploring the complexities of observing and responding to young children's communications of distress as they start day care', *Infant Observation*. Available at: https://doi.org/10.1080/13698036.2021.1875869

Brown, B. (2012) *Daring greatly: How the courage to be vulnerable transforms the way we live, love, parent and lead*. London: Portfolio Penguin.

Crozier, G. and Davies, J. (2007) 'Hard to reach parents or hard to reach schools? A discussion of home – school relations, with particular reference to Bangladeshi and Pakistani parents', *British Educational Research Journal*, 33(3), June, pp. 295–313.

Department for Education (2021) *Statutory framework for the early years foundation stage*. London: DfE.

Department for Education (DfE), England (2021a) *Statutory Framework for the early years foundation stage: Setting the standards for learning, development and care for children from birth to five*. Available at: https://assets.publishing.service.gov.uk/government/uploads/system/uploads/attachment_data/file/974907/EYFS_framework_-_March_2021.pdf

Department for Education (DfE), England (2021b) *Early years foundation stage profile: 2021 handbook*. Available at: https://assets.publishing.service.gov.uk/government/uploads/system/uploads/attachment_data/file/919681/Early_adopter_schools_EYFS_profile_handbook.pdf.

Department for Education (DfE) (England) (2021c) *Development matters: Non-statutory curriculum guidance for the early years foundation stage*. Available at: https://assets.publishing.service.gov.uk/government/uploads/system/uploads/attachment_data/file/971620/Development_Matters.pdf.

Dolby, R., Hughes, E. and Friezer, B. (2013) *Secure transitions: Supporting children to feel secure, confident, and included*. Canberra: Early Childhood Australia.

Early Education (2012) *Development matters in the early years foundation stage*. London: Early Education.

Early Years Coalition (2021) *Birth to 5 matters: Non-statutory guidance for the early years foundation stage, early education*. Available at: www.birthto5matters.org.uk/wp-content/uploads/2021/04/Birthto5Matters-download.pdf.

Elfer, P. (2012) 'Emotion in nursery work: Work discussion as a model of critical professional reflection', *Early Years: An International Journal of Research and Development*, 32(2), pp. 129–141.

Elfer, P. *et al.* (2018) *Froebel trust final evaluation report. Developing close, thoughtful attention to children and families in early years pedagogy: Evaluating the impact of Work Discussion Groups as a model of professional support and reflection.* Available at: www.froebel.org.uk/uploads/documents/Froebel-Trust-Elfer-et-al-2018-Work-Discussion-Evaluation-Final-Report-April-2018.pdf

Elfer, P. and Page, J. (2015) 'Pedagogy with babies: perspectives of eight nursery managers', *Early Child Development and Care*, 185(11–12), pp. 1762–1782.

Elfer, P. and Wilson, D. (2023) 'Talking with feeling: using Bion to theorise "work discussion" as a model of professional reflection with nursery practitioners', *Pedagogy, Culture & Society*, 31(1).

Fröbel, F., Michaelis, E. and Moore, H.K. (1915) *Autobiography of Friedrich Froebel.* Translated and annotated by Michaelis, E. and Moore, H.K., 1886 (Joint tr.). Print Book 1915 [12th ed.]. London: Allen & Unwin, p. 4.

Goldschmied, E. and Jackson, S. (1994) *People under three: Young children in day care.* London: Routledge.

Hopkins, J. (1988) 'Facilitating the development of intimacy between nurses and infants in day nurseries', *Early Child Development and Care*, 33(1–4), pp. 99–111. Available at: https://doi.org/10.1080/0300443880330108

Jackson, E. and Klauber, T. (2018) 'New developments: training in the facilitation of work discussion groups', *Infant Observation*, 21(2), pp. 241–260. Available at: https://doi.org/10.1080/13698036.2018.1559075

Knopf, H. and Swick, K. (2007) 'How parents feel about their child's teacher/school: Implications for early childhood professionals', *Early Childhood Education Journal*, 34(4), pp. 291–296.

Lilley, I. (1967) *Friedrich Froebel: A selection from his writings.* Cambridge: Cambridge University Press, p. 78.

Organisation for Economic Cooperation and Development (2017) *Starting strong: Key OECD indicators on early childhood education and care.* 21 June. Available at: https://www.oecd-ilibrary.org/education/starting-strong-2017_9789264276116-en

Page, J., Clare, A. and Nutbrown, C. (2013) *Working with babies and children from birth to three.* 2nd edn. London: Sage.

Page, J. and Elfer, P. (2013) 'The emotional complexity of attachment interactions in nursery', *European Early Childhood Education Research Journal*, 21(4), pp. 553–567.

Reid, S. (1997) *Developments in infant observation: The Tavistock model.* Edited by Susan Reid. London and New York: Routledge, p. 3.

Schön, D.A. (2016) *The reflective practitioner: How professionals think in action.* London: Routledge.

Souto-Manning, M. and Swick, K.J. (2006) 'Teachers' beliefs about parent and family involvement: Rethinking our family involvement paradigm', *Early Childhood Education Journal*, 34, pp. 187–193.

Tovey, H. (2020) *Froebel's principles and practice today.* London: Froebel Trust. Available at: www.froebel.org.uk/uploads/documents/FT-Froebels-principles-and-practice-today.pdf

Tronick, E. (2005) 'Why is connection with others so critical? Dyadic meaning making, messiness and complexity governed selective processes which co-create and expand individuals' state of consciousness', in Nadel, J. and Muir, D. (eds.) *Emotional development.* Oxford: Oxford University Press, pp. 293–315.

Urban, M. *et al.* (2012) 'Towards competent systems in early childhood education and care. Implications for policy and practice', *European Journal of Education*, 47(4), pp. 508–526.

Index